SAINT JOSEPH

HOLY WEEK MISSAL

The Complete English Text of All the
Masses and Ceremonies of the
New Holy Week Liturgy
from Palm Sunday to the
Easter Vigil Service

FOR CONGREGATIONAL USE

In accordance with the
Official Typical 1956 Edition of the
"Ordo Hebdomadæ Sanctæ Instauratus"

Introduction

OUR holy Mother the Church, appointed by God to teach all men, uses signs and symbols, vestments and lights, colors and ceremonies. They are all part of her role as an inspiring teacher, anxious to appeal to man's every sense to make her message clear and her mission complete.

Her liturgy, however, is not a mere drama at which men are silent spectators. Her liturgy appeals to men so that they might be moved to sentiments of love and adoration, thanksgiving and atonement.

She makes every Sunday the Lord's day, a reminder of Christ's victorious resurrection, the foundation of our faith and our hope Every Mass is "done in commemoration of Him," the unbloody renewal and living broad-ʳast of the Sacrifice of Calvary. Every day of the year ⸱ consecrates to God through this sacrifice, honoring he same time various mysteries of our Lord and sing God in His Mother and in His Saints.

3ut there is one whole week that is set apart for the ecial sanctification of men. It has been variously ᴧlled Painful Week, The Greater Week, and now the ᴧew Roman Ordo officially designates it as Hebdomada Sancta, Holy Week.

In quick succession Mother Church makes us assist at Christ's temporary triumph on Palm Sunday. She reads to us the various accounts of Christ's Passion. In a Solemn Evening Mass of the Last Supper she recalls

Nihil Obstat: RICHARD GINDER, S.T.L., Censor Librorum

Imprimatur: ✠ JOHN F. DEARDEN, Bishop of Pittsburgh

Pittsburgh, January 26, 1956

what St. Thomas considers to be "Christ's greatest miracle," the institution of the Holy Eucharist, and the first ordination of priests. She asks us to be near our Lord in His Agony, His Way of the Cross and Crucifixion, and invites us to receive the Victim in Holy Communion, not only on Holy Thursday but on Good Friday. And then, after a time of mourning from Friday to Saturday evening, she invites us to rise from the darkness to the light, during the ceremonies of the now restored Easter Vigil, in which Christ is symbolized by the Paschal Candle as the new Light, the Light of the world. She blesses baptismal water in which men can be buried with Christ and rise with Him, as children of God, and bids us renew our baptismal promises.

Finally, in a Midnight Mass she celebrates the dawn of Easter, honoring the Lord in all His glorious mysteries, and feeding her children once more with the flesh and blood of One Who is forever the Conqueror over death and sin, the Savior of all mankind.

Holy Week thus marks in a very special manner our ascent through Christ to God and God's descent through Christ to us. In both directions, He is the one Mediator, the Way, the Truth and the Life, joining earth to heaven, curing our weakness by His strength, cleansing our sinfulness by His holiness.

Truly this is the Greatest Week, the Holiest Week, in the Christian Year!

WALTER VAN DE PUTTE, C.S.Sp.

THE ORDINARY OF THE MASS

The Celebrant standing at the foot of the Altar, makes the proper reverence and, unless special rubrics direct otherwise, says in a loud voice:

IN THE Name of the Father, ✠ and of the Son, and of the Holy Ghost. Amen.

℣. I will go in to the altar of God.

The Ministers (or servers) respond:

℟. To God, the joy of my youth.

℣. Our help ✠ is in the name of the Lord.

℟. Who hath made heaven and earth.

Bowing down, the Celebrant says the "Confiteor."

℣ I confess to Almighty God, etc.

℟. May Almighty God have mercy on you, forgive you your sins, and bring you to life everlasting.

℣. Amen.

The Ministers (or servers) bow down and recite the "Confiteor."

I CONFESS to Almighty God, to Blessed Mary, ever Virgin, to Blessed Michael the Archangel, to Blessed John the Baptist, to the Holy Apostles Peter and Paul, and to all the Saints, and to you, Father, that I have sinned exceedingly in thought, word and deed, (*strike breast three times, saying:*) through my fault, through my fault, through my most grievous fault. Therefore I beseech Blessed Mary, ever Virgin, Blessed Michael the Archangel, Blessed John the Baptist, the Holy Apostles Peter and Paul, and all the Saints, and you, Father, to pray to the Lord our God for me.

℣ May Almighty God have mercy on you, forgive you your sins, and bring you to life everlasting.

℟. Amen.

Making the Sign of the Cross, the Celebrant says:

MAY the Almighty and Merciful Lord grant us pardon, ✠ absolution, and remission of our sins. ℟. Amen.

℣. Thou wilt turn, O God, and bring us life.
℟. And Thy people shall rejoice in Thee.
℣. Show us, O Lord, Thy mercy.
℟. And grant us Thy salvation.
℣. O Lord, hear my prayer.
℟. And let my cry come unto Thee.
℣. The Lord be with you.
℟. And with thy spirit.
℣. Let us pray.

Going up to the Altar, he says silently:

TAKE away from us our sins, O Lord, we beseech Thee, that we may enter with pure minds into the Holy of Holies. Through Christ our Lord. Amen.

Bowing down with hands joined on the Altar, he says:

WE BESEECH Thee, O Lord, by the merits of Thy Saints (*He kisses the Altar*) whose relics lie here, and of all the Saints: deign in Thy mercy to pardon me all my sins. Amen.

At Solemn Mass, and, on Holy Thursday, even at a sung Mass in the evening, the Celebrant blesses incense, saying:

Be thou blessed ✠ by Him in Whose honor thou shalt be consumed. Amen.

He then incenses the Altar and is in turn incensed by the Deacon.

At the Epistle side the Celebrant, making the Sign of the Cross, reads the "Introit," except on Good Friday and Holy Saturday.

THE INTROIT (Turn to Introit of Today's Mass)

THE KYRIE

Returning to the middle of the Altar, the Celebrant alternately with the Ministers (or servers), says:

℣. Lord, have mercy. ℟. Lord, have mercy. ℣. Lord, have mercy. ℟. Christ, have mercy. ℣. Christ, have mercy. ℟. Christ, have mercy. ℣. Lord, have mercy. ℟. Lord, have mercy. ℣. Lord, have mercy.

THE GLORIA

GLORY to God in the highest. And on earth peace to men of good will. We praise Thee. We bless Thee. We adore Thee. We glorify Thee. We give Thee thanks for Thy great glory. O Lord God, heavenly King, God the Father Almighty. O Lord Jesus Christ, the Only-begotten Son. O Lord God, Lamb of God, Son of the Father Who takest away the sins of the world, have mercy on us. Who takest away the sins of the world, receive our prayer. Who sittest at the right hand of the Father, have mercy on us. For Thou alone art holy. Thou alone art the Lord. Thou alone, O Jesus Christ, art most high. Together with the Holy Ghost ✠ in the glory of God the Father. Amen.

℣. The Lord be with you.

℞. And with thy spirit.

℣. Let us pray.

THE PRAYER (Turn to Prayer of Today's Mass)

After having read the prayer of the day, he continues to read the "Epistle," "Gradual," the "Tract" or "Alleluia" with versicle, according to the Season or Mass.

Prayer: CLEANSE MY HEART
Bowing down at the middle of the Altar, he says:

CLEANSE my heart and my lips, O Almighty God, Who didst cleanse the lips of the Prophet Isaias with a burning coal. In Thy gracious mercy deign so to purify me that I may worthily proclaim Thy holy Gospel. Through Christ our Lord. Amen.

Pray, Lord, Thy blessing.

The Lord be in my heart and on my lips, that I may worthily and fittingly proclaim His holy Gospel. Amen.

THE GOSPEL (Turn to Gospel of Today's Mass)

℣. The Lord be with you.

℟. And with thy spirit.

℣. ✠ The continuation (or the beginning) of the holy Gospel according to Saint *N*...

℟. Glory be to Thee, O Lord.

The Celebrant signs the book with the Sign of the Cross, and repeats this same sign on forehead, lips and breast.

After the "Gospel," the servers say: Praise be to Thee, O Christ. *The Celebrant, kissing the book, says:*

℣. By the words of the Gospel may our sins be taken away.

At Solemn Mass, when the history of our Lord's Passion is neither sung nor read (for, then the particular rubrics to be followed are inserted in their proper place), the Deacon places the Gospel book on the Altar and after the Celebrant blesses incense, he kneels and says the Prayer: 'Cleanse My Heart." He then takes the book, kneels before the Celebrant and asks his blessing, saying:

Father, grant thy blessing.

The Celebrant responds:

℣. **The Lord be in your heart and on your lips, that you may worthily and fittingly proclaim His holy Gospel: In the name of the Father, and of the Son, ✠ and of the Holy Ghost. Amen.**

After the Gospel, the Celebrant kisses the Gospel book, saying: By the words of the Gospel, may our sins be taken away, *and is then incensed by the Deacon.*

THE NICENE CREED

I BELIEVE in one God, the Father Almighty, Maker of heaven and earth, and of all things visible and invisible. And in one Lord Jesus Christ, the Only-begotten Son of God. Born of the Father before all ages. God of God; Light of Light; true God of true God. Begotten not made; of one being with the Father; by Whom all things were made. Who for us men, and for our salvation, came down from heaven. (*Here all genuflect.*) And was made Flesh by the Holy Ghost of the Virgin Mary: AND WAS MADE MAN. He was also crucified for us, suffered under Pontius Pilate and was buried. And on the third day He rose again according to the Scriptures. And ascending into heaven, He sitteth at the right hand of the Father. And He shall come again in glory to judge the living and the dead; and of His kingdom there shall be no end. And I believe in the Holy Ghost, Lord and Giver of life, Who proceeds from the Father and the Son. Who together with the Father and the Son is no less adored, and glorified: Who spoke by the Prophets. And I believe in One, Holy, Catholic and Apostolic Church. I confess one Baptism for the remission of sins. And I look for the resurrection of the dead. ✠ And the life of the world to come. Amen.

Having kissed the Altar, he turns to the people and says:

℣. The Lord be with you.

℟. And with thy spirit.

> *Then the Offertory antiphon, if any, is said.*

℣. Let us pray.

THE OFFERTORY (Turn to Offertory of Today's Mass)

> *At Solemn Mass, the Celebrant receives the paten with the host from the Deacon.*

OFFERTORY PRAYERS

ACCEPT, O Holy Father, Almighty and Eternal God, this spotless host, which I, Thy unworthy servant, offer unto Thee, my living and true God, to atone for my numberless sins, offenses, and negligences; on behalf of all here present and likewise for all faithful Christians living and dead, that it may profit me and them as a means of salvation unto life everlasting. Amen.

> *At Solemn Mass, the Deacon pours wine into the chalice and the Subdeacon pours the water which the Celebrant has blessed.*

O GOD, Who hast established the nature of man in wondrous dignity, and still more admirably restored it, grant that through the mystery of this water and wine, we may be made partakers of His Divinity, Who has condescended to become partaker of our humanity, Jesus Christ, Thy Son, our Lord. Who liveth and reigneth with Thee in the unity of the Holy Ghost, God, world without end. Amen.

Offering up the chalice, the Celebrant says:

WE OFFER Thee, O Lord, the chalice of salvation, humbly begging of Thy mercy that it may arise before Thy divine majesty, with a pleasing fragrance, for our salvation and for that of the whole world. Amen.

Then, making the Sign of the Cross with the chalice, and placing it on the corporal, he covers it with the pall.

At Solemn Mass, the Subdeacon receives the paten from the Deacon and covering it with the ends of the veil worn over his shoulders, he holds it before his eyes and takes his place at the foot of the Altar until the conclusion of the "Our Father."

Bowing down, the Celebrant says.

IN A humble spirit and with a contrite heart, may we be accepted by Thee, O Lord, and may our sacrifice so be offered in Thy sight this day as to please Thee, O Lord God.

Raising his eyes and blessing the Offering, he says:

COME, Thou Sanctifier, Almighty and Eternal God, and bless ✠ this sacrifice prepared for the glory of Thy holy name.

At Solemn Mass, and, on Holy Thursday, even at a sung Mass, the offerings of bread and wine are incensed, also the Altar and all who are present. The Celebrant blesses the incense, saying:

Through the intercession of Blessed Michael the Archangel, standing at the right hand of the altar of incense, and of all His elect may the Lord vouchsafe to bless ✠ this incense and to receive it in the odor of sweetness. Through Christ our Lord. Amen.

Receiving the thurible, he incenses the bread and wine, saying:

May this incense blessed by Thee, arise before Thee, O Lord, and may Thy mercy come down upon us.

Incensing the Altar, he says Psalm 140:

May my prayer be an incense-offering in Thy sight, my uplifted hands, as an evening sacrifice. Set, O Lord, a watch over my mouth, and a guard over the door of my lips. Permit not my heart to turn to evil, seeking pretexts for wickedness, with men who work iniquity.

Giving the thurible to the Deacon, he says:

May the Lord enkindle in us the fire of His love and the flame of everlasting charity. Amen.

The Celebrant is incensed, and after him, the Clergy, and then the whole congregation.

WASHING THE FINGERS

I WILL wash my hands among the innocent, and will walk 'round Thy altar, O Lord: To hear the voice of Thy praise and to tell all Thy wondrous deeds. Lord, I love the beauty of Thy house, and the place where Thy glory dwells. Destroy not my soul with the impious, O God, nor my life with men of blood. In whose hands there is iniquity, whose right hand is full of bribes. But as for me, I walk in my innocence, rescue me and be gracious to me. My foot is on the straight way, in assemblies will I bless Thee, O Lord.

On the Vigil of Easter (Holy Saturday) add the following:

Glory be to the Father, and to the Son, and to the Holy Ghost. As it was in the beginning, is now, and ever shall be, world without end. Amen.

Bowing down before the middle of the Altar, with hands joined, the Celebrant says:

ACCEPT, most holy Trinity, this offering which we are making to Thee in remembrance of the passion, resurrection, and ascension of Jesus Christ, our Lord, and in honor of Blessed Mary, ever Virgin, Blessed John the Baptist, the Holy Apostles Peter and Paul, and of these, and of all the Saints; that it may add to their honor and aid our salvation; and may they deign to intercede in heaven for us who honor their memory here on earth. Through the same Christ our Lord. Amen.

The Celebrant says audibly:

PRAY, brethren, that my sacrifice and yours may become acceptable to God the Father Almighty.

The sacred Ministers (or servers) or those assisting respond:

MAY the Lord accept this sacrifice from thy hands to the praise and glory of His name for our advantage, and that of all His holy Church. Amen.

The Celebrant recites the "Secret Prayer."

THE SECRET (Turn to Secret of Today's Mass)

At the end of the "Secret" the Celebrant says audibly:

Preface of the Holy Cross

The following Preface is sung or read in all Masses from the Second Sunday in Passion Time (Palm Sunday) up to Holy Thursday inclusive.

℣. World without end. ℟. Amen. ℣. The Lord be with you. ℟. And with thy spirit. ℣. Lift up your hearts. ℟. We have lifted them up unto the Lord. ℣. Let us give thanks to the Lord, our God. ℟. It is fitting and just.

IT IS fitting indeed and just, right and helpful to salvation, for us always and everywhere to give thanks to Thee, O Holy Lord, Father Almighty and Everlasting God; Who didst set the salvation of mankind upon the tree of the Cross, so that whence came death, thence also life might rise again, and he that overcame by the tree, by the tree also might be overcome: through Christ our Lord. Through Whom the angels praise Thy majesty, the dominions worship it, and the powers are in awe. The heavens and the heavenly Hosts, and the blessed seraphim join together in celebrating their joy. With these, we pray Thee, join our own voices also, while we say with lowly praise:

Here the bell rings three times:

HOLY, Holy, Holy, Lord God of Hosts. Heaven and earth are filled with Thy glory. Hosanna in the highest. Blessed is He Who comes in the name of the Lord. Hosanna in the highest.

THE CANON OF THE MASS

THEREFORE, most gracious Father, we humbly beg of Thee and entreat Thee through Jesus Christ Thy Son, our Lord, (*He kisses the Altar*) to deem acceptable and bless these ✠ gifts, these ✠ offerings, these ✠ holy and unspotted oblations which, in the first place, we offer Thee for Thy Holy Catholic Church, that Thou wouldst deign to give her peace and protection, to unite and guard her the whole world over, together with Thy servant *N...*, our Pope, and *N...*, our Bishop; and all true believers who cherish the Catholic and Apostolic Faith.

COMMEMORATION OF THE LIVING

REMEMBER, O Lord, Thy servants and handmaids, *N...* and *N...*,

He prays in particular for those he wishes to remember:
and all here present, whose faith and devotion are known to Thee, on whose behalf we offer to Thee or who themselves offer to Thee, this sacrifice of praise for themselves, families and friends, for the

good of their souls, for their hope of salvation and deliverance from all harm, and who offer their homage to Thee, O God, Eternal, Living and True.

COMMEMORATION OF THE SAINTS * †

IN THE unity of holy fellowship we observe the memory, first of all, of the glorious and ever Virgin Mary, Mother of our Lord and God Jesus Christ; next that of Thy Blessed Apostles and Martyrs, Peter and Paul, Andrew, James, John, Thomas, James, Philip, Bartholomew, Matthew, Simon and Thaddeus; of Linus, Cletus, Clement, Sixtus, Cornelius, Cyprian, Lawrence, Chrysogonus, John and Paul, Cosmas and Damian, and of all Thy Saints, by whose merits and prayers grant that we may be always fortified by the help of Thy protection. Through the same Christ our Lord. Amen. *The bell rings once:*

GRACIOUSLY accept, then, we beseech Thee, O Lord, this service of our worship and that of all Thy household. Order our days in Thy peace, save us from everlasting damnation, and cause us to be numbered among Thy chosen ones. Through Christ our Lord. Amen.

---

* ON THE EASTER VIGIL

IN THE unity of holy fellowship, and keeping the most holy night of the Resurrection of our Lord Jesus Christ according to the flesh; and also reverencing the memory first, of the glorious Mary, ever Virgin, Mother of our Lord and God Jesus Christ; next that, etc., *as above.*

GRACIOUSLY accept, then, we beseech Thee, O Lord, this service of our worship, and that of all Thy household, which we make unto Thee in behalf of those whom Thou hast vouchsafed to bring to a new birth by water and the Holy Ghost, giving them remission of all their sins; and dispose our days in Thy peace. Command that we be saved from eternal damnation, and be numbered in the flocks of those whom Thou hast chosen. Through Christ our Lord. Amen.

† *For the evening Mass on Holy Thursday, see page 67 for the "Commemoration of Saints" and following prayers.*

DO THOU, O God, deign to bless ✠ what we offer, and make it approved, ✠ effective, ✠ right, and wholly pleasing in every way, that it may become for our good, the Body ✠ and Blood ✠ of Thy dearly beloved Son, Jesus Christ our Lord.

CONSECRATION OF THE HOST

WHO, the day before He suffered, took bread into His holy and venerable hands, and having raised His eyes to heaven, unto Thee, O God, His Almighty Father, giving thanks to Thee, He blessed it, ✠ broke it, and gave it to His disciples, saying: Take ye all and eat of this:

For this is My Body.

When he elevates the Sacred Host, look at It and say· My Lord and My God!

CONSECRATION OF THE WINE

IN LIKE manner, when the supper was done, taking also this goodly chalice into His holy and venerable hands, again giving thanks to Thee, He blessed ✠ it, and gave it to His disciples, saying: Take ye all, and drink of this:

For this is the Chalice of My Blood of the new and eternal covenant; the mystery of faith, which shall be shed for you and for many unto the forgiveness of sins.

As often as you shall do these things, in memory of Me shall you do them.

The Celebrant adores the Precious Blood: you do likewise. The bell rings 3 times.

OFFERING THE VICTIM

MINDFUL, therefore, O Lord, not only of the blessed passion of the same Christ, Thy Son, our Lord, but also of His resurrection from the dead, and finally His glorious ascension into heaven, we, Thy ministers, as also Thy holy people, offer unto Thy supreme majesty, of Thy gifts bestowed upon us, the pure ✠ Victim, the holy ✠ Victim, the all-perfect ✠ Victim: the holy ✠ Bread of life eternal and the Chalice ✠ of unending salvation.

AND this do Thou deign to regard with gracious and kindly attention and hold acceptable, as Thou didst deign to accept the offerings of Abel, Thy just servant, and the sacrifice of Abraham our patriarch, and that which Thy chief priest Melchisedech offered unto Thee, a holy sacrifice and a spotless victim.

The Celebrant bows low.

MOST humbly we implore Thee, Almighty God, bid these offerings to be brought by the hands of Thy holy angel unto Thy altar above; before the face of Thy divine majesty; that those of us who, by sharing in the sacrifice of this altar, shall receive the most sacred ✠ Body and ✠ Blood of Thy Son, may be filled with every grace and heavenly blessing. Through the same Christ our Lord. Amen.

COMMEMORATION OF THE DEAD

REMEMBER also, O Lord, Thy servants and handmaids, *N*... and *N*..., who have gone before us with the sign of faith, and rest in the sleep of peace.

Here the Celebrant prays for such of the Dead as he wishes.

To these, O Lord, and to all who rest in Christ, we beseech Thee, to grant of Thy goodness, a place of comfort, light and peace. Through the same Christ our Lord. Amen.

Here, striking his breast and slightly raising his voice for the first three words, he says:

TO US sinners also, Thy servants, trusting in the greatness of Thy mercy, deign to grant some part and fellowship with Thy Holy Apostles and Martyrs: with John, Stephen, Matthias, Barnabas, Ignatius, Alexander, Marcellinus, Peter, Felicitas, Perpetua, Agatha, Lucy, Agnes, Cecilia, Anastasia, and all Thy Saints; into whose company, we implore Thee to admit us, not weighing our merits, but freely granting us pardon. Through Christ our Lord.

THROUGH Whom, O Lord, Thou dost always create, ✠ sanctify, ✠ fill with life, ✠ bless, and bestow upon us all good things.

THE MINOR ELEVATION

THROUGH ✠ Him, and with ✠ Him, and in ✠ Him, is to Thee, God the Father ✠ Almighty, in the unity of the Holy ✠ Ghost, all honor and glory.

℣. World without end. ℟. Amen.

SACRIFICIAL BANQUET

The Celebrant joins his hands, and says:

Let us pray.

Prompted by saving precepts, and taught by Thy divine teaching, we dare to say:

He extends his hands:

OUR Father, Who art in heaven, hallowed be Thy name: Thy kingdom come: Thy will be done on earth as it is in heaven. Give us this day our daily bread; and forgive us our trespasses, as we forgive those who trespass against us. And lead us not into temptation:

℟. But deliver us from evil. ℣. Amen.

He takes the paten between his first and second fingers, and says:

DELIVER us, we beseech Thee, O Lord, from all evils, past, present, and to come; and by the intercession of the Blessed and glorious Mary, ever Virgin, Mother of God, together with Thy

Blessed Apostles Peter and Paul, and Andrew, and all the Saints,

Making the Sign of the Cross on himself with the paten, he kisses it, and says:

grant of Thy goodness, peace in our days, that aided by the riches of Thy mercy, we may be always free from sin and safe from all disturbance.

The Celebrant genuflects and breaks the Sacred Host in two over the chalice. He places the portion in his right hand on the paten and breaks off a particle from the portion in his left hand, saying:

Through the same Jesus Christ, Thy Son, our Lord, Who liveth and reigneth with Thee in the unity of the Holy Ghost, God.

V. World without end.

R⁓. Amen.

V⁓. May the peace ✠ of the Lord be ✠ always with ✠ you.

He puts the particle into the chalice, saying:

MAY this mingling and consecration of the Body and Blood of our Lord Jesus Christ help us who receive it unto life everlasting. Amen.

Striking his breast three times, he says:

LAMB of God, Who takest away the sins of the world, have mercy on us.

Lamb of God, Who takest away the sins of the world, have mercy on us.

Lamb of God, Who takest away the sins of the world, grant us peace.

In the Evening Mass on Holy Thursday, "Have mercy on us" is repeated for the third time. On Holy Saturday this threefold invocation is omitted.

Prayers BEFORE HOLY COMMUNION

In the Evening Mass on Holy Thursday and in the Mass on the Vigil of Easter, the Kiss of Peace is not given and the following prayer is omitted.

O LORD Jesus Christ, Who hast said to Thy Apostles: Peace I leave you, My peace I give you: regard not my sins but the faith of Thy

Church, and deign to give her peace and unity according to Thy will: Who livest and reignest God, world without end. Amen.

At Solemn Mass, the Celebrant kisses the Altar, and giving the Pax (Kiss of Peace) to the Deacon, says: Peace be with you. *To which the Deacon answers:* And with thy spirit.

O LORD Jesus Christ, Son of the living God, Who, by the will of the Father, with the co-operation of the Holy Ghost, hast by Thy death given life to the world, deliver me by this Thy most sacred Body and Blood from all my sins and from every evil. Make me always cling to Thy commandments, and never permit me to be separated from Thee. Who with the same God the Father and the Holy Ghost, livest and reignest, God, world without end. Amen.

LET not the partaking of Thy Body, O Lord Jesus Christ, which I, though unworthy, presume to receive, turn to my judgment and condemnation; but through Thy goodness, may it become a safeguard and an effective remedy, both of soul and body. Who livest and reignest with God the Father, in the unity of the Holy Ghost, God, world without end. Amen.

I will take the Bread of heaven, and call upon the name of the Lord.

Slightly inclining, he takes both parts of the Sacred Host and paten in his left hand; then, striking his breast with his right hand, and raising his voice a little, he says three times (the bell rings each time):

LORD, I am not worthy that Thou shouldst come under my roof; but only say the word, and my soul will be healed.

He then makes the Sign of the Cross with the Sacred Host, holding It in his right hand over the paten, saying:

MAY the Body of our Lord Jesus Christ keep my soul unto life everlasting. Amen.

He then reverently consumes the Host, joins his hands, and remains a short time in prayer. Then he uncovers the chalice, makes a genuflection, collects whatever particles may remain and puts them in the chalice, saying:

WHAT return shall I make to the Lord for all He hath given me? I will take the chalice of salvation, and I will call upon the name of the Lord. Praising will I call upon the Lord and I shall be saved from my enemies.

Making the Sign of the Cross with the chalice, he says:

MAY the Blood of our Lord Jesus Christ keep my soul unto life everlasting. Amen.

COMMUNION OF THE FAITHFUL

Servers say the "Confiteor," page 4.

At Solemn Mass, if there are communicants, the Deacon says the "Confiteor."

MAY Almighty God have mercy on you, forgive you your sins, and bring you to life everlasting. R̶. Amen.

V̶. May the Almighty and Merciful Lord grant you pardon, ✠ absolution and remission of your sins. R̶. Amen.

Holding up a Sacred Host and turning toward the people, the Celebrant says:

Behold the Lamb of God, behold Him Who takes away the sins of the world.

Lord, I am not worthy that Thou shouldst come under my roof; but only say the word, and my soul will be healed. (3 *times.*)

The Celebrant goes to the Altar rail and administers Holy Communion, saying to each person:

May the Body of our Lord Jesus Christ preserve your soul unto life everlasting. Amen.

The Celebrant replaces the ciborium in the Tabernacle. He then purifies the chalice with a little wine, saying:

WHAT has passed our lips as food, O Lord, may we possess in purity of heart, that what is given to us in time, be our healing for eternity.

Then purifying his fingers with wine and water, he says:

MAY Thy Body, O Lord, which I have eaten, and Thy Blood which I have drunk, cleave unto my very soul, and grant that no trace of sin be found in me, whom these pure and holy mysteries have renewed. Who livest and reignest world without end. Amen.

He takes the ablution, wipes his lips, and chalice, which he covers, and places in the middle of the Altar.

COMMUNION AND POSTCOMMUNION *(Turn to Communion and Postcommunion of Today's Mass)*

Having said the Communion verse the Celebrant kisses the Altar, and turning to the people, says: The Lord be with you. R. And with thy spirit. V. Let us pray. *At the end of the Postcommunion the response is:* R. Amen.

FINAL PRAYERS

℣. The Lord be with you. ℟. And with thy spirit.

The Celebrant turns to the Altar and, according to the rubrics, says either Go, you are dismissed, *or* Let us bless the Lord. R. Thanks be to God. *But in the Mass on the Vigil of Easter, is said:* Go, you are dismissed, alleluia, alleluia. R. Thanks be to God, alleluia, alleluia.

At Solemn Mass, the Deacon sings: Go you are dismissed, *or* Let us bless the Lord, etc.

MAY the tribute of my worship be pleasing to Thee, most holy Trinity, and grant that the sacrifice which I, all unworthy, have offered in the presence of Thy majesty, may be acceptable to Thee, and through Thy mercy obtain forgiveness for me and all for whom I have offered it. Through Christ our Lord. Amen.

THE BLESSING

Then he kisses the Altar, and raising his eyes, and extending, raising, and joining his hands, he bows his head, and then facing the congregation gives the blessing. At the Evening Solemn or Sung Mass on Holy Thursday, the blessing is not given.

MAY Almighty God bless you: ✠ the Father, and the Son, and the Holy Ghost. Amen.

THE LAST GOSPEL

℣ The Lord be with you. ℟. And with thy spirit.

℣. ✠ The beginning of the Holy Gospel according to St. John. ℟. Glory be to Thee, O Lord.

IN THE beginning was the Word, and the Word was with God; and the Word was God. He was in the beginning with God. All things were made through Him, and without Him was made nothing that has been made. In Him was life, and the life was the light of men. And the light shines in the darkness; and the darkness grasped it not. There was a man, one sent from God, whose name was John. This man came as a witness, to bear witness concerning the Light, that all might believe through Him. He was not himself the Light, but was to bear witness to the Light. It was the true Light that enlightens every man who comes into the world. He was in the world, and the world was made by Him, and the world knew Him not. He came unto His own, and His own received Him not. But to as many as received Him He gave the power of becoming sons of God; to those who believe in His Name: who were born not of blood, nor of the will of the flesh, nor of the will of man, but of God. AND THE WORD WAS MADE FLESH, (*Here all genuflect*) and dwelt among us. And we saw His glory, the glory as of the Only-begotten of the Father, full of grace and of truth.

℟. Thanks be to God.

HOLY WEEK

During this, the holiest week of the year, Mother Church asks her children to recall with singular devotion the greatest mysteries of our faith: "Christ crucified, buried and then risen," and also Christ instituting the Most Holy Eucharist. In order to make it easier for the faithful to participate in those inspiring and grace-laden ceremonies, Pope Pius XII promulgated the following Order for Holy Week.

SECOND SUNDAY IN PASSION TIME
OR PALM SUNDAY

Dbl. 1st Cl.   Red and Purple

This Sunday commemorates Christ's triumphal entrance into Jerusalem. For this reason the Church blesses palms to remind us of the multitude which accompanied Him carrying branches and strewing them in His way, while they chanted: "Hosanna to the Son of David! Blessed is He Who comes in the name of the Lord! Hosanna in the highest!"

The Blessing, the Antiphons of the Procession and the *"Hymn to Christ the King"* make this one of the most impressive ceremonies of the Liturgical Year.

SOLEMN PROCESSION OF THE PALMS
IN HONOR OF CHRIST THE KING

The Blessing of Palms

At a convenient hour, the Celebrant, omitting the usual Asperges and sprinkling with holy water, blesses the Palms, olive branches or branches of other trees.

The color of the vestments is red.

The Celebrant is vested in amice, alb, cincture, stole and cope; the Deacon, with amice, alb, cincture, stole and dalmatic; the Subdeacon, with amice, alb, cincture and tunicle.

(When there are no Deacon and Subdeacon, the Celebrant vests in amice, alb, cincture, stole and cope, or else without the chasuble.)

The Palms, unless the faithful already are holding them, are prepared on a credence table, covered with a white cloth and placed in a suitable place in the sanctuary, so that it is in full view of the people.

Then the Celebrant, with the Ministers (or servers), after genuflecting before the Altar, stands behind the credence table, facing the people. Meanwhile the following antiphon is sung:

Antiphon. *Matt. 21, 9.* Hosanna to the Son of David! Blessed is He Who comes in the name of the Lord. O King of Israel: Hosanna in the highest.

Then the Celebrant, his hands joined, blesses the Palm branches, singing in a ferial tone:

℣. Dóminus vobíscum. | ℣. The Lord be with you.

To which all respond:

℟. Et cum spíritu tuo. | ℟. And with thy spirit.

In the following prayer the Celebrant says, according to the type of Palm branches used, "branches of Palm," "branches of olive, or other trees," etc.

Let us pray. Bless, ✠ we beseech Thee, O Lord, these branches of Palm (or olive, or other trees), and grant that, what Thy people today bodily perform for Thy honor, they may spiritually perfect with the utmost devotion, by gaining the victory over the enemy, and ardently loving every work of mercy. Through our Lord, etc. S. Amen.

Then the Celebrant first sprinkles three times the Palm branches placed on the credence table, then, going to the Altar railing, the Palms of the people, if they already are holding them, unless he prefers to bless these by walking around the aisles of the church.

Thereupon, the Celebrant puts incense into the thurible in the usual manner and incenses the blessed Palm branches on the credence table three times, then those held by the people, or else he incenses the Palms held by the people by walking around the aisles of the church.

The sacred Ministers (or servers) assist the Celebrant in the aspersion and incensation, holding the edges of his cope.

The Distribution of Palms

After the blessing, the Palms are distributed according to the local custom.

Accordingly, the Celebrant standing on the predella of the Altar, facing the people, and assisted by the sacred Ministers (or servers), distributes the blessed Palms first to the Clergy, according to rank, then to the servers, and lastly, to the people at the Altar railing.

When he begins to distribute the Palms, the following antiphons and psalms are sung:

1st Antiphon. The Hebrew children, bearing olive branches, went forth to meet the Lord, crying out and saying: Hosanna in the highest.

Ps. 23, 1-2, 7-10. The Lord's are the earth and its fullness, the world and those who dwell in it.

For He founded it upon the seas, and established it upon the rivers.

The 1st antiphon is repeated: The Hebrew children, etc.

Lift up, O gates, your lintels; reach up, you ancient portals, that the king of glory may come in!

"Who is this king of glory?" "The Lord, strong and mighty, the Lord, mighty in battle."

The 1st antiphon is repeated: The Hebrew children, etc.

Lift up, O gates, your lintels; reach up, you ancient portals, that the king of glory may come in!

"Who is this king of glory?" "The Lord of hosts; He is the king of glory."

The 1st antiphon is repeated: The Hebrew children, etc.

Glory be to the Father, and to the Son, and to the Holy Ghost, as it was in the beginning is now and ever shall be, world without end. Amen.

The 1st antiphon is repeated: The Hebrew children, etc.

2nd Antiphon. The Hebrew children spread their garments in the way, and cried out, saying: Hosanna to the Son of David; blessed is He Who comes in the name of the Lord.

Ps. 46. All you people, clap your hands, shout to God with cries of gladness.

For the Lord, the Most High, the awesome, is the great king over all the earth.

The 2nd antiphon is repeated: The Hebrew children, etc.

He brings peoples under us; nations under our feet.

He chooses for us our inheritance, the glory of Jacob, whom he loves.

The 2nd antiphon is repeated: The Hebrew children, etc.

God mounts His throne amid shouts of joy; the Lord, amid trumpet blasts.

Sing praise to God, sing praise; sing praise to our king, sing praise.

The 2nd antiphon is repeated: The Hebrew children, etc.

For king of all the earth is God; sing hymns of praise.

God reigns over the nations, God sits upon His holy throne.

The 2nd antiphon is repeated: The Hebrew children, etc.

The princes of the peoples are gathered together with the people of the God of Abraham.

For God's are the guardians of the earth; He is supreme.

The 2nd antiphon is repeated: The Hebrew children, etc.

Glory be to the Father, and to the Son, and to the Holy Ghost, as it was in the beginning, is now and ever shall be, world without end. Amen.

The 2nd antiphon is repeated: The Hebrew children, etc.

The above psalms and antiphons are repeated if the distribution of Palms is still in progress; but, if the distribution of Palms ends before the last verse of Psalm 46, the chanting is ended with the "Glory be" and the antiphon is repeated.

The Reading of the Gospel

When the distribution of Palms has ended and the credence table has been removed, the Celebrant washes his hands in silence; then, ascending the Altar, he kisses it in the middle and puts incense into the thurible in the usual manner. The Deacon places the Gospel book on the Altar, and everything is done in the same manner as at the time of singing the Gospel, page 7.

(When there are no Deacon and Subdeacon, the Celebrant does everything in the same manner as in a sung Mass, page 6.)

Gospel. *Matt. 21, 1-9.* At that time, when Jesus drew near to Jerusalem, and came to Bethphage, on the Mount of Olives, He sent two disciples, saying to them, "Go into the village opposite you, and immediately you will find an ass tied, and a colt with her; loose them and bring them to Me. And if anyone say anything to you, you shall say that the Lord has need of them, and immediately he will send them." Now this was done that what was spoken through the prophet might be fulfilled, "Tell the daughter of Sion: Behold, thy King comes to thee, meek and seated upon an ass, and upon a colt, the foal of a beast of burden." So the disciples went and did as Jesus had directed them. And they brought the ass and the colt, laid their cloaks on them, and made Him sit thereon. And most of the crowd spread their cloaks upon the road, while others were cutting branches from the trees, and strewing them on the road. And the crowds that went before Him, and those that followed, kept crying out, saying, "Hosanna to the Son of David! Blessed is He Who comes in the name of the Lord!" (S. Praise be to Thee, O Christ.)

At the end of the Gospel the Subdeacon presents the book to the Celebrant for him to kiss. The Celebrant is not incensed by the Deacon.

The Procession with the Blessed Palms

The Celebrant puts incense into the thurible in the usual manner. Then, the Deacon, turning toward the people, says:

℣. Procedámus in pace. | ℣. Let us go forth in peace.

All respond:

℟. In nómine Christi. Amen. | ℟. In the name of Christ. Amen.

The Procession now takes place. The Thurifer leads, carrying the thurible, then another vested Subdeacon, or Acolyte (or one of the servers), carrying the unveiled Cross, flanked by two Acolytes (or servers) with lighted candlesticks; the Clergy, in order of rank, follows, and lastly, the Celebrant with Deacon and Subdeacon; after these, the people, carrying Palms.

The Procession follows, if possible, a somewhat longer route outside the church. If there is another church in which the blessing of Palms can be performed conveniently, there is nothing that prohibits this taking place there, and then the Procession can proceed to the principal church.

At the beginning of the Procession all or some of the following antiphons may be sung as time permits.

1st Antiphon. The multitude goes forth to meet the Redeemer with flowers and palms, and pays the homage due to a triumphant Conqueror; the Gentiles proclaim the Son of God; and their voices thunder through the skies in praise of Christ: Hosanna.

2nd Antiphon. Let the faithful join with the Angels and children, singing to the Conqueror of death: Hosanna in the highest.

3rd Antiphon. The great multitude that was gathered together at the festival acclaimed the Lord, "Blessed is He Who comes in the name of the Lord: Hosanna in the highest."

4th Antiphon. *Luke 19, 37-38.* The whole company of those descending began to rejoice and to praise God with a loud voice for all the miracles that they had seen, saying, "Blessed is He Who comes as King, in the name of the Lord! Peace on earth, and glory in the highest!"

During the Procession the following hymn is sung by the people, if possible, repeating the first two verses as noted.

Hymn to Christ the King

Choir: Glória, laus et honor tibi sit, Rex Christe Redémptor, cui pueríle decus prompsit Hosánna pium.

Glory, praise and honor to Thee, O Christ our King, the Redeemer: to Whom children sang their glad and sweet hosanna's.

All: Glória, laus, etc.

Glory, praise, etc.

Choir: Israël es tu Rex, Davídis et ínclita proles, nómine qui in Dómini, Rex benedícite, venis.

Hail, King of Israel! David's Son of royal fame! Who comest in the name of the Lord, O blessed King.

All: Glória, laus, etc.

Glory, praise, etc.

Choir: Cœtus in excélsis te laudat cǽlicus omnis, et mortális homo, et cuncta creáta simul.

The Angel host praise Thee on high, on earth mankind, with all created things.

All: Glória, laus, etc.

Glory, praise, etc.

Choir: Plebs Hebrǽa tibi cum palmis óbvia venit; cum prece, voto, hymnis, ádsumus ecce tibi.

With palms the Hebrew people went forth to meet Thee. We greet Thee now with prayers and hymns.

All: Glória, laus, etc.

Glory, praise, etc.

Choir: Hi tibi passúro solvébant múnia laudis; nos tibi regnánti pángimus ecce melos.

On Thy way to die, they crowned Thee with praise; we raise our song to Thee, now King on high.

All: Glória, laus, etc.

Glory, praise, etc.

Choir: Hi placuére tibi, pláceat devótio nostra: Rex bone, Rex clemens, cui bona tuncta placent.

Their poor homage pleased Thee, O gracious King! O clement King, accept ours too, the best that we can bring.

All: Glória, laus, etc.

Glory, praise, etc.

5th Antiphon. All acclaim Thy name, and say, "Blessed is He Who comes in the name of the Lord: Hosanna in the highest."

Psalm 147

Glorify the Lord, O Jerusalem, praise your God, O Sion. For He has strengthened the bars of your gates, He has blessed your children within you. He has granted peace in your borders, with the best of wheat He fills you. He sends forth His command to the earth, swiftly runs His word! He spreads snow like wool, frost He strews like ashes. He scatters His hail like crumbs, before His cold the waters freeze. He sends His word and melts them, He lets His breeze blow and the waters run. He has proclaimed His word to Jacob, His statutes and His ordinances to Israel. He has not done thus for any other nation, His ordinances He has not made known to them. Glory be, etc.

5th Antiphon. Let all acclaim and say, "Blessed is He Who comes in the name of the Lord."

6th Antiphon. With glistening Palms we prostrate ourselves before the Lord as He approaches: we all run to Him with hymns and canticles, glorifying and saying: "Blessed is the Lord."

7th Antiphon. Hail, our King, Son of David, Redeemer of the world, Whom the prophets predicted would come as a Savior to the house of Israel. For the Father has sent Thee into the world as its saving Victim, Whom all the holy ones expected from the beginning of the world, and now:

"Hosanna to the Son of David. Blessed is He Who comes in the name of the Lord. Hosanna in the highest."

As the Procession enters the church and the Celebrant passes through the doors of the church, the last antiphon is begun.

8th Antiphon. As the Lord entered the holy city, the Hebrew children declaring the resurrection of Life, carrying Palm branches, cried out: "Hosanna in the highest."

When the people heard that Jesus was coming to Jerusalem, they went forth to meet Him.

Carrying Palm branches, they cried out: "Hosanna in the highest."

When the Celebrant reaches the foot of the Altar, he genuflects and ascends the Altar with the sacred Ministers. Standing between the Ministers and facing the people, he says, with hands joined, in a ferial tone, the prayer that ends the Procession, while a Cleric holds the book.

(When there are no Deacon and Subdeacon, the servers take the place of the Ministers in assisting with the book, and all is done as described above.)

℣. Dóminus vobíscum. | ℣. The Lord be with you.

All respond:

℟. Et cum spíritu tuo. | ℟. And with thy spirit.

Let us pray. O Lord Jesus Christ, our King and Redeemer, in Whose honor we have sung solemn praises while carrying these branches, grant we beseech Thee, that, wherever these branches may be carried, there, may the grace of Thy blessing descend, and every iniquity and deceit of the devils being routed, may Thy right hand protect those whom it has redeemed. Who livest, etc. ℟. Amen.

At the end of the prayer, the Celebrant and Ministers genuflect, leave the Altar, remove their red vestments and put on purple vestments for the Mass.

Palm branches are not held while the history of the Lord's Passion is sung or read during Mass.

THE MASS

Station: St. John Lateran

The color of the vestments is purple. The sacred Ministers put on the dalmatic and tunicle. The same is repeated on Monday, Tuesday and Wednesday.

Where the Blessing and Procession of Palm branches has taken place before Mass, the Celebrant comes to the Altar with the sacred Ministers (or servers) and, omitting the prayers at the foot of the Altar, immediately ascends, kisses the middle of the Altar and incenses it as usual.

Introit. *Ps. 21, 20. 22.* O Lord, remove not Thy help afar from me; look to my defense: deliver me from the lion's mouth, and my lowness from the horns of the unicorns. *Ps. 21, 2.* O God, my God, look upon me; why hast Thou forsaken me? Far from my salvation, are the words of my sins. —O Lord, remove not.

● *Kyrie, page 5. Omit Gloria.*

Prayer. Almighty and everlasting God, Who didst will that our Savior should take upon Himself our flesh, and suffer on the Cross, that all mankind might have His example of humility for their imitation: grant that we may merit both to keep in mind the lesson of His patience, and to be made partakers of His Resurrection. Through the same, etc. S. Amen.

Epistle. *Phil. 2, 5-11.* Brethren: Have this mind in you which was also in Christ Jesus, Who though He was by nature God, did not consider being equal to God a thing to be clung to, but emptied Himself, taking the nature of a slave and being made like unto men. And appearing in the form of man, He humbled Himself, becoming obedient to death, even to death on a cross. Therefore God has exalted Him and has bestowed upon Him the Name that is above every name, so that at the Name of Jesus every knee should bend of those in heaven, on earth and under the earth, and every tongue should confess that the Lord Jesus

Christ is in the glory of God the Father. S. Thanks be to God. ⤳

Gradual. *Ps. 72, 24. 1-3.* Thou hast held me by my right hand; and by Thy will Thou hast conducted me; and with glory Thou hast received me. ℣. How good is God to Israel, to those who are of a right heart! But my feet were almost moved, my steps had well-nigh slipped; because I had a zeal on occasion of sinners, seeing the peace of sinners. ⤳

Tract. *Ps. 21, 2-9. 18. 19. 22. 24. 32.* O God, my God, look upon me: why hast Thou forsaken me? ℣. Far from my salvation, are the words of my sins. ℣. O my God, by day shall I cry, and Thou wilt not hear; and by night, and it shall not be reputed as folly in me. ℣. But Thou dwellest in the holy place, the praise of Israel. ℣. In Thee have our fathers hoped: they have hoped, and Thou hast delivered them. ℣. They cried to Thee, and they were saved: they trusted in Thee, and were not confounded. ℣. But I am a worm, and no man: the reproach of men, and the outcast of the people. ℣. All they who saw me, laughed me to scorn: they spoke with their lips, and wagged their heads. ℣. He hoped in the Lord, let Him deliver him: let Him save him, seeing he delights in Him. ℣. But they looked and stared upon me: they parted my garments amongst them, and upon my vesture they cast lots. ℣. Deliver me from the lion's mouth: and my lowliness from the horns of the unicorns. ℣. You who fear the Lord, praise Him: all you the seed of Jacob, glorify Him. ℣. There shall be declared to the Lord a generation to come: and the heavens shall show forth His justice. ℣. To a people that shall be born, which the Lord has made.

After the reading of the Epistle, uncovered lecterns are placed on the Gospel side of the sanctuary and the history of the Lord's Passion is sung or read as follows:

It must be sung or read by Ministers who are at least ordained Deacons. Assisted by two Acolytes (or servers), without candles or incense, they proceed to the Altar, and, kneeling on the lowest step, they make a profound bow and recite in a low voice the prayer, "Cleanse my heart," page 6, and ask the Celebrant's blessing, saying, "Pray Father, thy blessing." The Celebrant, turning toward them, answers in medium voice:

May the Lord be in your hearts and on your lips, that you may worthily and fittingly proclaim His holy Gospel: in the name of the Father, and of the Son, ✠ and of the Holy Ghost.

And they say: Amen.

Then, together with the Acolytes (or servers), they genuflect and go to the lecterns; they neither sign the book nor themselves with the Sign of the Cross, while they begin to sing or to read.

(When there are no Deacon and Subdeacon, the Celebrant, after having read the Gradual and Tract, says, as usual in the middle of the Altar, "Cleanse my heart," "Pray, Father," and "May the Lord be in my heart." Then, on the Gospel side of the Altar, he reads or sings the history of the Lord's Passion in a clear voice, but does not sign the book nor himself with the Sign of the Cross, while he begins to read or sing.)

This manner of singing or reading is also observed on Tuesday and Wednesday, when the history of the Lord's Passion is sung or read.

The three Deacons sing or read the history of the Lord's Passion as follows: the first, called the Chronicler, sings or reads the narrative parts; the second, called the Synagogue, the words of any other person; and the third, the words of Christ. The same is repeated for Tuesday, Wednesday and Good Friday.

PASSION OF OUR LORD JESUS CHRIST
Matthew 26, 36-75; 27, 1-54

AT THAT time, Jesus came with His disciples to a country place called Gethsemani, and He said to His disciples, "Sit down here, while I go over yonder and pray." And He took with Him

Peter and the two sons of Zebedee, and He began to be saddened and exceedingly troubled. Then He said to them, "My soul is sad, even unto death. Wait here and watch with Me." And going forward a little, He fell prostrate and prayed, saying, "Father, if it is possible, let this cup pass away from Me; yet not as I will, but as Thou willest." Then He came to the disciples and found them sleeping. And He said to Peter, "Could you not, then, watch one hour with Me? Watch and pray, that you may not enter into temptation. The spirit indeed is willing, but the flesh is weak." Again a second time He went away and prayed, saying, "My Father, if this cup cannot pass away unless I drink it, Thy will be done." And He came again and found them sleeping, for their eyes were heavy. And leaving them He went back again, and prayed a third time, saying the same words over. Then He came to His disciples, and said to them, "Sleep on now, and take your rest! Behold, the hour is at hand when the Son of Man will be betrayed into the hands of sinners. Rise, let us go. Behold, he who betrays Me is at hand."

And while He was yet speaking, behold Judas, one of the Twelve, came and with him a great crowd with swords and clubs, from the chief priests and elders of the people. Now His betrayer had given them a sign, saying, "Whomever I kiss, that is He; lay hold of Him." And he went straight up to Jesus and said, "Hail, Rabbi!" and kissed Him. And Jesus said to him, "Friend, for what purpose hast thou come?" Then they came forward and set hands on Jesus and took Him. And behold, one of those who were with Jesus, reached out his hand, drew his sword, and struck the servant of the high priest, cutting off his ear. Then Jesus said to him, "Put back thy sword into its place; for all those who take the sword will perish by the sword. Or dost thou suppose that I cannot entreat My Father, and He will even now furnish Me with more than twelve legions of angels? How then are the Scriptures to be fulfilled, that thus it must take place?"

In that hour Jesus said to the crowds, "As against a robber you have come out, with swords and clubs, to seize Me. I sat daily with you in the temple teaching, and you did not lay hands on Me." Now all this was done that the Scriptures of the prophets might be fulfilled. Then all the disciples left Him and fled.

Now those who had taken Jesus led Him away to Caiphas the high priest, where the Scribes and the elders had gathered together. But Peter was following Him at a distance, even to the court-yard of the high priest, and he went in and sat with the attendants to see the end. Now the chief priests and all the Sanhedrin were seeking false witness against Jesus, that they might put Him to death, but they found none, though many false witnesses came forward. But last of all two false witnesses came forward, and said, "This man said, 'I am able to destroy the temple of God, and to rebuild it after three days.'" Then the high priest, standing up, said to Him, "Dost Thou make no answer to the things that these men prefer against Thee?" But Jesus kept silence. And the high priest said to Him, "I adjure Thee by the living God that Thou tell us whether Thou art the Christ, the Son of God." Jesus said to him. "Thou hast said it. Nevertheless, I say to you, hereafter you shall see the Son of Man sitting at the right hand of the Power and coming upon the clouds of heaven." Then the high priest tore his garments, saying, "He has blasphemed; what further need have we of witnesses? Behold, now you have heard the blasphemy. What do you think?" And they answered and said, "He is liable to death."

Then they spat in His face and buffeted Him; while others struck His face with the palms of their hands, saying, "Prophesy to us, O Christ! who is it that struck Thee?" Now Peter was sitting outside in the courtyard; and a maidservant came up to him and said, "Thou also wast with Jesus the Galilean." But he denied it before them all, saying, "I do not know what thou art saying." And when he had gone out to the gateway, another maid saw him, and said to those who were there, "This man also was with Jesus of Nazareth." And again he denied it with an oath, "I do not know the man!" And after a little while the bystanders came up and said to Peter, "Surely thou also art one of them, for even thy speech betrays thee." Then he began to curse and to swear that he did not know the man. And at that moment a cock crowed. And Peter remembered the word that Jesus had said, "Before a cock crows, thou wilt deny Me three times." And he went out and wept bitterly.

Now when morning came all the chief priests and the elders of the people took counsel together against Jesus in order to put Him to death. And they bound Him and led Him away, and delivered Him to Pontius Pilate the procurator. Then Judas, who betrayed Him, when he saw that He was condemned, repented and brought back the thirty pieces of silver to the chief priests and the elders, saying, "I have sinned in betraying innocent blood." But they said, "What is that to us? See to it thyself." And he flung the pieces of silver into the temple, and withdrew; and went away and hanged himself with a halter. And the chief priests took the pieces of silver, and said, "It is not lawful to put them into the treasury, seeing that it is the price of blood." And after they had consulted together, they bought with them the potter's field, as a burial place for strangers. For this reason that field has been called even to this day, Haceldama, that is, the Field of Blood. Then what was spoken through Jeremias the prophet was fulfilled, "And they took the thirty pieces of silver, the price of Him Who was priced, upon Whom the children of Israel set a price; and they gave them for the potter's field, as the Lord directed me."

Now Jesus stood before the procurator, and the procurator asked Him, saying, "Art Thou the king of the Jews?" Jesus said to him, "Thou sayest it." And when He was accused by the chief priests and the elders, He made no answer. Then Pilate said to Him, "Dost Thou not hear how many things they prefer against Thee?" But He did not answer him a single word, so that the procurator wondered exceedingly. Now at festival time the procurator used to release to the crowd a prisoner, whomever they would. Now he had at that time a notorious prisoner called Barabbas. Therefore, when they had gathered together, Pilate said, "Whom do you wish that I release to you? Barabbas, or Jesus who is called Christ?" For he knew that they had delivered Him up out of envy. Now, as he was sitting on the judgment-seat, his wife sent to him, saying, "Have nothing to do with that just Man, for I have suffered many things in a dream today because of Him." But the chief priests and the elders persuaded the crowds to ask for Barabbas and to destroy Jesus. But the procurator addressed them, and said to them, "Which of the two do you wish that I release to you?" And they said, "Barabbas." Pilate said to them, "What then am I to do with Jesus Who is called Christ?" They all said, "Let Him be crucified!" The procurator said to them, "Why, what evil has He done?" But they kept crying out the more, saying, "Let Him be crucified!" Now Pilate, seeing that he was doing no good, but rather that a riot was breaking out, took water and washed his hands in sight of the crowd, saying, "I am innocent of the blood of this just Man; see to it yourselves." And all the people answered and said, "His blood be on us and on our children." Then he released to them Barabbas; but Jesus he scourged and delivered to them to be crucified.

Then the soldiers of the procurator took Jesus into the prætorium, and gathered together about Him the whole cohort. And they stripped Him and put on Him a scarlet cloak; and plaiting a crown of thorns, they put it upon His head, and a reed into His right hand; and bending the knee before Him they mocked Him, saying, "Hail, King of the Jews!" And they spat on Him, and took the reed and kept striking Him on the head. And when they had mocked Him, they took the cloak off Him and put His own garments on Him, and led Him away to crucify Him.

Now as they went out, they found a man of Cyrene named Simon; him they forced to take up His Cross. And they came to the place called Golgotha, that is, the Place of the Skull. And they gave Him wine to drink mixed with gall; but when He had tasted it, He would not drink. And after they had crucified Him, they divided His garments, casting lots, [to fulfill what was spoken through the prophet, "They divided My garments among them, and upon My vesture they cast lots."] And sitting down they kept watch over Him. And they put above His head the charge against Him, written, "This is Jesus, the King of the Jews."

Then two robbers were crucified with Him, one on His right hand and one on His left. Now the passers-by were jeering at Him, shaking their heads, and saying, "Thou Who destroyest the temple, and in three days buildest it up again, save Thyself! If Thou art the Son of God, come down from the Cross!" In like manner, the chief priests with the Scribes and the elders, mocking, said, "He saved others, Himself He cannot save! If He is the King of Israel, let Him come down now from the Cross, and we will believe Him. He trusted in God; let Him deliver Him now, if He wants Him; for He said, 'I am the Son of God.'"

And the robbers also, who were crucified with Him, reproached Him in the same way.

Now from the sixth hour there was darkness over the whole land until the ninth hour. But about the ninth hour Jesus cried out with a loud voice, saying, "Eli, Eli, lamma sabacthani," that is, "My God, My God, why hast Thou forsaken Me?" And some of the bystanders on hearing this said, "This man is calling Elias." And immediately one of them ran and, taking a sponge, soaked it in common wine, put it on a reed and offered it to Him to drink. But the rest said, "Wait, let us see whether Elias is coming to save Him." But Jesus again cried out with a loud voice, and gave up His spirit. *(Here all kneel and pause a few moments.)*

And behold, the curtain of the temple was torn in two from top to bottom; and the earth quaked, and the rocks were rent, and the tombs were opened, and many bodies of the saints who had fallen asleep arose; and coming forth out of the tombs after His Resurrection, they came into the Holy City, and appeared to many. Now when the centurion, and those who were with him keeping guard over Jesus, saw the earthquake and the things that were happening, they were very much afraid, and they said, "Truly He was the Son of God." And many women were there, looking on from a distance, who had followed Jesus from Galilee, ministering to Him. Among them were Mary Magdalene, and Mary the mother of James and Joseph, and the mother of the sons of Zebedee.

Now when it was evening, there came a certain rich man of Arimathea, Joseph by name, who was himself a disciple of Jesus. He went to Pilate and asked for the body of Jesus. Then Pilate ordered the body to be given up. And Joseph taking the body, wrapped it in a clean linen cloth, and laid it in his new tomb, which he had hewn out in the rock. Then he rolled a large stone to the entrance of the tomb, and departed. S. Praise be to Thee, O Christ.

After singing or reading the history of the Lord's Passion, the Celebrant does not kiss the book, nor is he incensed. This is also observed on Tuesday, Wednesday and Good Friday, when the history of the Lord's Passion is sung or read.

Those who celebrate a second or third Mass today are not bound to repeat the reading of the Lord's Passion; in place of it the following Gospel is read in the usual manner:

Gospel. *Matt. 27, 45-52.* After they had crucified Jesus, from the sixth hour there was darkness over the whole land until the ninth hour. But about the ninth hour Jesus cried out with a loud voice, saying, "Eli, Eli, lamma sabacthani," that is, "My God, my God, why hast Thou forsaken Me?" And some of the bystanders on hearing this said, "This man is calling Elias." And immediately one of them ran and, taking a sponge, soaked it in common wine, put it on a reed and offered it to Him to drink. But the rest said, "Wait, let us see whether Elias is coming to save Him." But Jesus again cried out with a loud voice, and gave up His spirit. *(Here all kneel and pause a few moments.)* And behold, the curtain of the temple was torn in two from top to bottom; and the earth quaked, and the rocks were rent, and the tombs were opened, and many bodies of the saints who had fallen asleep arose. S. Praise be to Thee, O Christ.

● *Creed, page 7.*

Offertory. *Ps. 68, 21-22.* My heart has expected reproach and misery; and I looked for one who would grieve together with Me, and there was none; I sought one who would comfort Me, and found none; and they gave Me gall for My food, and in My thirst they gave Me vinegar to drink.

● *Offertory Prayers, page 8.*

Secret. Grant, we beseech Thee, O Lord, that

the gift now offered in the sight of Thy Majesty, may obtain for us both the grace of devotion, and that everlasting happiness which is our aim. Through our Lord, etc.

- *Preface of the Holy Cross, page* 11.

Communion. *Matt. 26, 42.* Father, if this cup cannot pass away, unless I drink it, Thy will be done.

℣. The Lord be with you. ℞. And with thy spirit. ↱

Postcommunion. By the working of this mystery, O Lord, may our vices be cleansed and our just desires be fulfilled. Through our Lord, etc. ℞. Amen.

- *Final Prayers, page* 20. *Omit Last Gospel.*

In the remaining Masses without the blessing of Palm branches, the Gospel, page 26, is read at the end.

MONDAY IN HOLY WEEK

Priv. Feria, Simple   *Station: St. Praxedes*   Purple

- *Beginning of Mass, page* 4.

Introit. *Ps. 34, 1-2.* Judge Thou, O Lord, those who wrong me, overthrow those who fight against me; take hold of arms and shield, and rise up to help me, O Lord, the strength of my salvation. *Ps. 34, 3.* Bring out the sword, and shut up the way against those who persecute me; say to my soul: I am thy salvation.—Judge Thou, O Lord.

- *Kyrie, page 5. Omit Gloria.*

Prayer. Grant, we beseech Thee, almighty God, that we, who fail through our weakness in so many difficulties, may be relieved through the pleading of the Passion of Thy Only-begotten Son. Who with Thee liveth, etc. ℞. Amen. ↱

Epistle. *Isa. 50, 5-10.* In those days, Isaias said: The Lord God has opened my ear, and I do not resist: I have not gone back. I have given my body to the strikers, and my cheeks to those who plucked them; I have not turned away my face from those who rebuked me and spit upon me. The Lord God is my helper, therefore am I not confounded: therefore have I set my face as a most hard rock, and I know that I shall not be confounded. He is near Who justifies me. Who will contend with me? Let us stand together. Who is my adversary? Let him come near to me. Behold the Lord God is my helper: who is he who shall condemn me? Lo, they shall be destroyed as a garment, the moth shall eat them up. Who is there among you who fears the Lord, who hears the voice of His servant, who has walked in darkness, and has no light? Let him hope in the name of the Lord and lean upon his God. ℞. Thanks be to God. ⇒

Gradual. *Ps. 34, 23. 3.* Arise, O Lord, and be attentive to my judgment, to my cause, my God and my Lord. ℣. Bring out the sword, and shut up the way against those who persecute me. ⇒

Tract. *Ps. 102, 10.* O Lord, repay us not according to the sins we have committed, nor according to our iniquities. ℣. *Ps. 78, 8. 9.* O Lord, remember not our former iniquities, let Thy mercies speedily prevent us: for we are become exceeding poor. *(Here kneel.)* ℣. Help us, O God, our Savior: and for the glory of Thy name, O Lord, deliver us: and forgive us our sins for Thy name's sake.

• *Prayer: Cleanse My Heart, page 6.*

Gospel. *John 12, 1-9.* Six days before the Passover, Jesus came to Bethany where Lazarus, whom Jesus had raised to life, had died. And they made Him a supper there; and Martha served, while Lazarus was one of those reclining at table with Him. Mary therefore took a pound of ointment, genuine nard of great value, and anointed the feet of Jesus, and with her hair wiped His feet dry. And the house was filled with the odor of the ointment. Then one of His disciples, Judas Iscariot, he who was about to betray Him, said, "Why was this ointment not sold for three hundred denarii, and given to the poor?" Now he said this, not that he cared for the poor, but because he was a thief, and holding the purse, used to take what was put in it. Jesus therefore said, "Let her be—that she may keep it for the day of My burial. For the poor you have always with you, but you do not always have Me." Now the great crowd of the Jews learned that He was there; and they came, not only because of Jesus, but that they might see Lazarus, whom He had raised from the dead. ℞. Praise be to Thee, O Christ.

℣. The Lord be with you. ℞. And with thy spirit. ➚

Offertory. *Ps. 142, 9. 10.* Deliver me from my enemies, O Lord; to Thee have I fled, teach me to do Thy will, for Thou art my God.

• *Offertory Prayers, page* 8.

Secret. Grant, almighty God, that being cleansed by the powerful virtue of these sacrifices, we may come with greater purity to their divine source. Through our Lord, etc.

• *Preface of the Holy Cross, page* 11.

Communion. *Ps. 34, 26.* Let them blush and be ashamed together, who rejoice at my evils: let them be clothed with shame and fear, who speak malignant things against me.

℣. The Lord be with you. ℞. And with thy spirit. ➚

Postcommunion. Let Thy holy rites, O Lord, impart to us divine fervor; that we may delight both in their celebration and in their fruit. Through our Lord, etc. ℞. Amen. ➚

Prayer Over The People. Let us pray. Bow down your heads before God.

Help us, O God, our Savior; and grant that we may celebrate with joy the memory of those benefits by which Thou didst deign to redeem us. Through our Lord, etc. *S.* Amen.

- *Final Prayers, page* 20.

TUESDAY IN HOLY WEEK

Priv. Feria, Simple   *Station: St. Prisca*   Purple

- *Beginning of Mass, page* 4.

Introit. *Gal. 6, 14.* But it behooves us to glory in the Cross of our Lord Jesus Christ: in Whom is our salvation, life, and resurrection; by Whom we are saved and delivered. *Ps. 66, 2.* May God have mercy on us, and bless us: may He cause the light of His countenance to shine upon us; and may He have mercy on us.—But it behooves.

- *Kyrie, page* 5. *Omit Gloria.*

Prayer. O almighty and everlasting God, grant us so to celebrate the mysteries of the Lord's Passion, that we may deserve to obtain Thy pardon. Through the same, etc. *S.* Amen. ꜋

Epistle. *Jer. 11, 18-20.* In those days, Jeremias said: O Lord, Thou hast shown me, and I have known: then Thou didst show me their doings. And I was as a meek lamb that is carried to be a victim: and I knew not that they had devised counsels against me, saying: Let us put wood on his bread and cut him off from the land of the living, and let his name be remembered no more. But Thou, O Lord of Sabaoth, Who judgest justly, and triest the reins and the hearts, let me see Thy revenge on them: for to Thee have I revealed my cause, O Lord my God. *S.* Thanks be to God. ꜋

Gradual. *Ps. 34, 13. 1-2.* But as for me, when they were troublesome to me, I was clothed with haircloth, and I humbled my soul with fasting, and my prayer shall be turned into my bosom. ℣. Judge Thou, O Lord, those who wrong me, overthrow those who fight against me, take hold of arms and shield, and rise up to help me.

For the reading of the Passion, the same rubrics are observed as on page 33.

PASSION OF OUR LORD JESUS CHRIST
Mark 14, 32-72; 15, 1-46

AT THAT time, Jesus and His disciples came to a country place called Gethsemani, and He said to His disciples, "Sit down here, while I pray." And He took with Him Peter and James and John, and He began to feel dread and to be exceedingly troubled. And He said to them, "My soul is sad, even unto death. Wait here and watch." And going forward a little, He fell on the ground, and began to pray that, if it were possible, the hour might pass from Him; and He said, "Abba, Father, all things are possible to Thee. Remove this cup from Me; yet not what I will, but what Thou willest." Then He came and found them sleeping. And He said to Peter, "Simon, dost thou sleep? Couldst thou not watch one hour? Watch and pray, that you may not enter into temptation. The spirit indeed is willing, but the flesh is weak." And again He went away and prayed, saying the same words over. And He came again and found them sleeping, for their eyes were heavy. And they did not know what answer to make to Him. And He came the third time, and said to them, "Sleep on now, and take your rest! It is enough; the hour has come. Behold, the Son of Man is betrayed into the hands of sinners. Rise, let us go. Behold, he who will betray Me is at hand." And while He was yet speaking, Judas Iscariot, one of the Twelve, came and with him a great crowd with swords and clubs, from the chief priests and the Scribes and the elders. Now His betrayer had given them a sign, saying, "Whomever I kiss, that is He; lay hold of Him, and lead Him safely away." And when he came, he went straight up to Him, and said, "Rabbi!" and kissed Him. And they seized Him and held Him. But one of the bystanders drew his sword, and struck the servant of the high priest, and cut off his ear. And Jesus, addressing them, said, "As against a robber you have come out, with swords and clubs, to seize Me. I was daily with you in the temple teaching, and you did not lay hands on Me. But it is so that the Scriptures may be fulfilled." Then all His disciples left Him and fled. And a certain young man was following Him, having a linen cloth wrapped about his naked body, and they seized him. But leaving the linen cloth behind, he fled away from them naked.

And they led Jesus away to the high priest; and all the priests and the Scribes and the elders gathered together. But Peter followed Him at a distance, even to the courtyard of the high priest, and was sitting with the attendants at the fire and warming himself. Now the chief priests and all the Sanhedrin were seeking witness against Jesus, that they might put Him to death, but they found none. For while many bore false witness against Him, their evidence did not agree. And some stood up and bore false witness against Him, saying, "We ourselves have heard Him say, 'I will destroy this temple built by hands, and after three days I will build another, not built by hands.'" And even then their evidence did not agree. Then the high priest, standing up in their midst, asked Jesus, saying, "Dost Thou make no answer to the things that these men prefer against Thee?" But He kept silence, and made no answer. Again the high priest began to ask Him, and said to Him, "Art Thou the Christ, the Son of the Blessed One?" And Jesus said to him, "I am. And you shall see the Son of Man sitting at the right hand of the Power and coming with the clouds of heaven." But the high priest tore his garments and said, "What further need have we of witnesses? You have heard the blasphemy. What do you think?" And they all condemned Him as liable to death.

And some began to spit on Him, and to blindfold Him, and to buffet Him, and to say to Him, "Prophesy." And the attendants struck Him with blows of their hands.

And while Peter was below in the courtyard, there came one of the maidservants of the high priest; and seeing Peter warming himself, she looked closely at him and said, "Thou also wast with Jesus of Nazareth." But he denied it, saying, "I neither know nor understand what thou art saying." And he went outside into the vestibule; and the cock crowed. And the maidservant, seeing him again, began to say to the bystanders, "This is one of them." But again he denied it. And after a little while the bystanders again said to Peter, "Surely thou art one of them, for thou art also a Galilean." But he began to curse and to swear: "I do not know this Man you are talking about." And at that moment a cock crowed a second time. And Peter remembered the word that Jesus had said to him, "Before a cock crows twice, thou wilt deny Me three times." And he began to weep.

And as soon as it was morning, the chief priests held a consultation with the elders, the Scribes and the whole Sanhedrin. And they bound Jesus and led Him away, and delivered Him to Pilate. And Pilate asked Him, "Art Thou the king of the Jews?" and He answered him and said, "Thou sayest it." And the chief priests accused Him of many things. And Pilate again asked Him, saying, "Hast Thou no answer to make? Behold how many things they accuse Thee of." But Jesus made no further answer, so that Pilate wondered.

Now at festival time he used to release to them one of the prisoners, whomever they had petitioned for. Now there was a man called Barabbas imprisoned with some rioters, one who in the riot had committed murder. And the crowd came up, and began to ask that he do for them as he was wont. But Pilate addressed them, saying, "Do you wish that I release to you the King of the Jews?" For he knew that the chief priests had delivered Him up out of envy. But the chief priests stirred up the crowd to have him release Barabbas for them instead. But Pilate again spoke and said to them, "What then do you want me to do to the King of the Jews?" But they cried out again, "Crucify Him!" But Pilate said to them, "Why, what evil has He done?" But they kept crying out the more, "Crucify Him!" So Pilate, wishing to satisfy the crowd, released to them Barabbas; but Jesus he scourged and delivered to be crucified.

Now the soldiers led Him away into the courtyard of the prætorium, and they called together the whole cohort. And they clothed Him in purple, and plaiting a crown of thorns, they put it upon Him, and began to greet Him, "Hail, King of the Jews!" And they kept striking Him on the head with a reed, and spitting upon Him; and bending their knees, they did homage to Him. And when they had mocked Him, they took the purple off Him and put His own garments on Him, and led Him out to crucify Him. And they forced a certain passer-by, Simon of Cyrene, coming from the country, the father of Alexander and Rufus, to take up His Cross.

And they brought Him to the place called Golgotha, which, translated, is the Place of the Skull. And they gave Him wine to drink mixed with myrrh; but He did not take it. Then they crucified Him, and divided His garments, casting lots for them to see what each should take. Now it was the third hour and they crucified Him. And the inscription bearing the charge against Him was, "The King of the Jews." And they crucified two robbers with Him, one on His right hand and one on His left. And the Scripture was fulfilled, which says, "And He was reckoned among the wicked." And the passers-by were jeering at Him, shaking their heads, and saying, "Aha, Thou Who destroyest the temple, and in three days buildest it up again; come down from the Cross, and save Thyself!" In like manner, the chief priests with the Scribes said in mockery to one another, "He saved others, Himself He cannot save! Let the Christ, the King of Israel, come down now from the Cross, that we may see and believe." And they who were crucified with Him reproached Him. And when the sixth hour came, there was darkness over the whole land until the ninth hour. And at the ninth hour Jesus cried out with a loud voice, saying, "Eloi, Eloi, lamma sabacthani?" which, translated, is, "My God, my God, why hast Thou forsaken me?" And some of the bystanders on hearing this said, "Behold, He is calling Elias." But someone ran, soaked a sponge in common wine, put it on a reed and offered it to Him to drink, saying, "Wait, let us see whether Elias is coming to take Him down." But Jesus cried out with a loud voice, and expired. *(Kneel and pause a few moments.)*

And the curtain of the temple was torn in two from top to bottom. Now when the centurion, who stood facing Him, saw how He had thus cried out and expired, he said, "Truly this Man was the Son of God." And some women were also there, looking on from a distance. Among them were Mary Magdalene, Mary the mother of James the Less and of Joseph, and Salome. These used to accompany Him and minister to Him when He was in Galilee—besides many other women who had come with Him to Jerusalem.

Now when it was evening, as it was the Day of Preparation, that is, the eve of the Sabbath, there came Joseph of Arimathea, a councillor of high rank, who was himself looking for the kingdom of God. And he went in boldly to Pilate and asked for the body of Jesus. But Pilate wondered whether He had already died. And sending for the centurion, he asked him whether He was already dead. And when he learned from the centurion that He was, he granted the body to Joseph. And Joseph bought a linen cloth, and took Him down, and wrapped Him in the linen cloth, and laid Him in a tomb which had been hewn out of a rock. Then he rolled a stone to the entrance of the tomb. ℟. Praise be to Thee, O Christ.

℣. The Lord be with you. ℟. And with thy spirit. ➘

Offertory. *Ps. 139, 5.* Keep me, O Lord, from the hand of the wicked, and from unjust men deliver me.

• *Offertory Prayers, page 8.*

Secret. May these sacrifices, O Lord, we beseech Thee, which are instituted with healing fasts, speedily restore us. Through our Lord, etc.

• *Preface of the Holy Cross, page 11.*

Communion. *Ps. 68, 13. 14.* They who sat in the gate were busied against me; and they who drank wine made me their song. But as for me, my prayer is to Thee, O Lord; for the time of Thy good pleasure, O God, in the multitude of Thy mercy.

℣. The Lord be with you. ℟. And with thy spirit. ➘

Postcommunion. May our vices be cured, almighty God, by Thy holy mysteries, and may we receive everlasting healing. Through, etc. ℟. Amen.

Prayer Over The People. Let us pray. Bow down your heads before God.

May Thy mercy, O God, cleanse us from the deceits of our old nature, and enable us to be formed anew unto holiness. Through our Lord, etc.

• *Final Prayers, page 20.*

WEDNESDAY IN HOLY WEEK

Priv. Feria, Simple   *Station: St. Mary Major*   Purple

• *Beginning of Mass, page 4.*

Introit. *Phil. 2, 10. 8. 11.* At the Name of Jesus every knee should bend, of those in heaven, on earth and under the earth, for the Lord became obedient unto death, even to death on a Cross. Therefore our Lord Jesus Christ is in the glory of God the Father. *Ps. 101, 2.* O Lord, hear my prayer, and let my cry come to Thee.—At the Name.

• *Kyrie, page 5. Omit Gloria.*

Let us pray. Let us kneel. ℟. Arise.

Prayer. Grant, we beseech Thee, O almighty God, that we, who are continually afflicted through our excesses and sins, may be delivered by the Passion of Thy Only-begotten Son. Who with Thee, etc. ℟. Amen. ⮧

Lesson. *Isa. 62, 11; 63, 1-7.* Thus saith the Lord God: Tell the daughter of Sion: Behold thy Savior comes; behold His reward is with Him and His work before Him. Who is this that comes from Edom, with dyed garments from Bosra, this beautiful one in his robe, walking in the greatness of his strength? I, that speak justice and am a defender to save. Why then is thy apparel red, and thy garments like theirs that tread in the winepress? I have trodden the winepress alone, and of the Gentiles there is not a man with me: I have trampled on them in my indignation and have trodden them down in my wrath; and their blood is sprinkled upon my garments, and I have stained all my apparel. For the day of vengeance is in my heart, the year of my redemption is come. I looked about, and there was none to help: I sought, and there was none to give aid: and my own arm has saved for me, and my indignation itself has helped me. And I have trodden down the people in my wrath and have made them drunk in my indignation, and have brought down their strength to the earth. I will remember the tender mercies of the Lord, the praise of the Lord for all the things that the Lord our God has bestowed upon us. R̤. Thanks be to God. ⟩

Gradual. *Ps. 68, 18. 2-3.* Turn not away Thy face from Thy servant, for I am in trouble: hear me speedily. V̤. Save me, O God, for the waters are come in even unto my soul: I stick fast in the mire of the deep, and there is no sure standing.

V. The Lord be with you. R̤. And with thy spirit. ⟩

Prayer. O God, Who didst will that Thy Son should suffer for us the ignominy of the Cross to deliver us from the power of the enemy, grant to us Thy servants, that we may attain to the grace of the resurrection. Through the same, etc. R̤. Amen. ⟩

Epistle. *Isa. 53, 1-12.* In those days, Isaias said: Who has believed our report, and to whom is the arm of the Lord revealed? And He shall grow up as a tender plant before Him, and as a root out of a thirsty ground; there is no beauty in Him, nor comeliness; and we have seen Him, and there was no sightliness that we should be desirous of Him; despised and the most abject of men, a man of sorrows and acquainted with infirmity; and His look was as it were hidden and despised, whereupon we esteemed Him not. Surely He has borne our infirmities and carried our sorrows: and we have thought Him as it were a leper, and as one struck by God and afflicted. But He was wounded for our iniquities, He was bruised for our sins; the chastisement of our peace was upon Him, and by His bruises we are healed. All we like sheep have gone astray, everyone has turned aside into his own way: and the Lord has laid on Him the iniquity of us all. He was offered because it was His own will, and He opened not His mouth: **He shall be led as a sheep to the slaughter, and shall be dumb as a lamb before his shearer, and He shall not open His mouth.** He was taken away from distress and from judgment: who shall declare His generation? Because He is cut off out of the land of the living: for the wickedness of My people have I struck Him. And He shall give the ungodly for His burial, and the rich for His death, because He has done no iniquity, neither was there deceit in His mouth. And the Lord was pleased to bruise Him in infirmity; if He shall lay down His life for sin, He shall see a long-lived seed, and the will of the Lord shall be prosperous in His hand. Because His soul has labored, He shall see and be filled: by His knowledge shall this My just servant justify many, and He shall bear their iniquities. Therefore will I distribute to Him very many, and He shall divide the spoils of the strong, because He has delivered His soul unto death and was reputed with the wicked: and has borne the sins of many and has prayed for the transgressors. ℟. Thanks be to God. ❧

Tract. *Ps. 101, 2-5. 14.* Hear, O Lord, my prayer, and let my cry come to Thee. ℣. Turn not away Thy face from me: in the day when I am in trouble, incline Thy ear to me. ℣. In whatever day I shall call upon Thee, hear me speedily. ℣. For my days are vanished like smoke; and my bones are burnt up as in an oven. ℣. I am smitten like the grass, and my heart is withered: because I forgot to eat my bread. ℣. Thou shalt arise, O Lord, and have mercy on Sion: for the time is come to have mercy on it.

For the reading of the Passion, the same rubrics are observed as on page 33.

PASSION OF OUR LORD JESUS CHRIST

Luke 22, 39-71; 23, 1-53

AT THAT time, Jesus came out and went, according to His custom, to the Mount of Olives, and the disciples also followed Him. But when He was at the place, He said to them, "Pray, that you may not enter into temptation." And He Himself withdrew from them about a stone's throw, and kneeling down, He began to pray, saying, "Father, if Thou art willing, remove this cup from Me; yet not My will but Thine be done." And there appeared to Him an angel from heaven to strengthen Him. And falling into an agony He prayed the more earnestly. And His sweat became as drops of blood running down upon the ground. And rising from prayer He came to the disciples, and found them sleeping for sorrow. And He said to them, "Why do you sleep? Rise and pray, that you may not enter into temptation."

And while He was yet speaking, behold, a crowd came; and he who was called Judas, one of the Twelve, was going before them, and he drew near to Jesus to kiss Him. But Jesus said to him, "Judas, dost thou betray the Son of Man with a kiss?" But when they who were about Him saw what would follow, they said to Him, "Lord, shall we strike with the sword?" And one of them struck the servant of the high priest and cut off his right ear. But Jesus answered and said, "Bear with them thus far." And He touched his ear and healed him. But Jesus said to the chief priests and captains of the temple and elders, who had come against Him, "As against a robber have you come out, with swords and clubs. When I was daily with you in the temple, you did not stretch forth your hands against Me. But this is your hour, and the power of darkness."

Now having seized Him, they led Him away to the high priest's house; but Peter was following at a distance. And when they had kindled a fire in the middle of the courtyard, and were seated together, Peter was in their midst. But a certain maidservant saw him sitting at the blaze, and after gazing upon him she said, "This man too was with Him." But he denied Him, saying, "Woman, I do not know Him." And after a little while someone else saw him and said, "Thou, too, art one of them." But Peter said, "Man, I am not." And about an hour later another insisted, saying, "Surely this man, too, was with Him, for he also is a Galilean." But Peter said, "Man, I do not know what thou sayest." And at that moment, while he was yet speaking, a cock crowed. And the Lord turned and looked upon Peter. And Peter remembered the word of the Lord, how He said, "Before a cock crows, thou wilt deny Me three times." And Peter went out and wept bitterly.

And the men who had Him in custody began to mock Him and beat Him. And they blindfolded Him, and kept striking His face and asking Him, saying, "Prophesy, who is it that struck Thee?" And many other things they kept saying against Him, reviling Him.

And as soon as day broke, the elders of the people and the chief priests and Scribes gathered together; and they led Him away into their Sanhedrin, saying, "If Thou art the Christ, tell us." And He said to them, "If I tell you, you will not believe Me; and if I question you, you will not answer Me, or let Me go. But henceforth, the Son of Man will be seated at the right hand of the power of God." And they all said, "Art Thou, then, the Son of God?" He answered, "You yourselves say that I am." And they said, "What further need have we of witnesses? For we have heard it ourselves from His own mouth."

And the whole assemblage rose, and took Him before Pilate. And they began to accuse Him, say-

ing, "We have found this man perverting our nation, and forbidding the payment of taxes to Cæsar,
and saying that He is Christ a king." So Pilate
asked Him, saying, "Art Thou the king of the
Jews?" And He answered him and said, "Thou
sayest it." And Pilate said to the chief priests and
to the crowds, "I find no guilt in this Man." But
they persisted, saying, "He is stirring up the people,
teaching throughout all Judea, and beginning from
Galilee even to this place."

But Pilate, hearing Galilee, asked whether the
Man was a Galilean. And learning that He belonged
to Herod's jurisdiction, he sent Him back to Herod,
who likewise was in Jerusalem in those days.
Now when Herod saw Jesus, he was exceedingly
glad; for he had been a long time desirous to see
Him, because he had heard so much about Him,
and he was hoping to see some miracle done by
Him. Now he put many questions to Him, but He
made him no answer. Now the chief priests and
Scribes were standing by, vehemently accusing
Him. But Herod, with his soldiery, treated Him
with contempt and mocked Him, arraying Him in
a bright robe, and sent Him back to Pilate. And
Herod and Pilate became friends that very day;
whereas previously they had been at enmity with
each other. And Pilate called together the chief
priests and the rulers and the people, and said to
them, "You have brought before me this Man, as
one who perverts the people; and behold, I upon
examining Him in your presence have found no
guilt in this Man as touching those things of which
you accuse Him. Neither has Herod; for I sent you
back to him, and behold, nothing deserving of
death has been committed by Him. I will therefore
chastise Him and release Him."

Now at festival time it was necessary for him to
release to them one prisoner. But the whole mob
cried out together, saying, "Away with this Man,
and release to us Barabbas!"—one who had been

thrown into prison for a certain riot that had occurred in the city, and for murder. But Pilate spoke to them again, wishing to release Jesus. But they kept shouting, saying, "Crucify Him! Crucify Him!" And he said to them a third time, "Why, what evil has this Man done? I find no crime deserving of death in Him. I will therefore chastise Him and release Him." But they persisted with loud cries, demanding that He should be crucified; and their cries prevailed. And Pilate pronounced sentence that what they asked for should be done. So he released to them him who for murder and riot had been put in prison, for whom they were asking; but Jesus he delivered to their will.

And as they led Him away, they laid hold of a certain Simon of Cyrene, coming from the country, and upon him they laid the Cross to bear it after Jesus. Now there was following Him a great crowd of the people, and of women, who were bewailing and lamenting Him. But Jesus turning to them said, "Daughters of Jerusalem, do not weep for Me, but weep for yourselves and for your children. For behold, days are coming in which men will say, 'Blessed are the barren, and the wombs that never bore, and breasts that never nursed.' Then they will begin to say to the mountains, 'Fall upon us,' and to the hills, 'Cover us!' For if in the case of green wood they do these things, what is to happen in the case of the dry?"

Now there were also two other malefactors led to execution with Him. And when they came to the place called the Skull, they crucified Him there, and the robbers, one on His right hand and the other on His left. And Jesus said, "Father, forgive them, for they do not know what they are doing." Now in dividing His garments, they cast lots. And the people stood looking on; and the rulers with them kept sneering at Him, saying, "He saved others; let Him save Himself, if He is the Christ, the Chosen One of God." And the soldiers also mocked Him, coming to Him and offering Him common wine, and saying, "If Thou art the King of the Jews, save Thyself." And there was also an inscription written over Him in Greek and Latin and Hebrew letters, "This is the King of the Jews." Now one of those robbers who were hanged was abusing Him, saying, "If Thou art the Christ, save Thyself and us!" But the other in answer rebuked him and said, "Dost not even thou fear God, seeing that thou art under the same sentence? And we indeed justly, for we are receiving what our deeds deserved; but this man has done nothing wrong." And he said to Jesus, "Lord, remember me when Thou comest into Thy kingdom." And Jesus said to him, "Amen I say to thee, this day thou shalt be with Me in paradise."

It was now about the sixth hour, and there was darkness over the whole land until the ninth hour. And the sun was darkened, and the curtain of the temple was torn in the middle. And Jesus cried out with a loud voice and said, "Father, into Thy hands I commend My spirit." And having said this, He expired. (Here all kneel for a few moments.)

Now when the centurion saw what had happened, he glorified God, saying, "Truly this was a just Man." And all the crowd that collected for the sight, when they beheld what things had happened, began to return beating their breasts. But all His acquaintances, and the women who had followed Him from Galilee, were standing at a distance looking on.

And behold, there was a man named Joseph, a councillor, a good and just man—he had not been party to their plan of action—of Arimathea, a town of Judea, who was himself looking for the kingdom of God. He went to Pilate and asked for the body of Jesus. And he took Him down, and wrapped Him in a linen cloth, and laid Him in a rock-hewn tomb where no one had ever yet been laid. ℟. Praise be to Thee, O Christ.

℣. The Lord be with you. ℟. And with thy spirit. ◥

Offertory. *Ps. 101, 2. 3.* Hear, O Lord, my prayer: and let my cry come to Thee; turn not away Thy face from me.

  • *Offertory Prayers, page 8.*

Secret. Receive, O Lord, we beseech Thee, the gift which we offer, and in Thy mercy, grant that we may obtain by loving affection wnat we celebrate in this mystery of the Passion of Thy Son our Lord. Through the same, etc.

  • *Preface of the Holy Cross, page 11.*

Communion. *Ps. 101, 10. 13. 14.* I mingled my drink with weeping, for having lifted me up Thou hast thrown me down, and I am withered like grass; but Thou, O Lord, endurest forever: Thou shalt arise and have mercy on Sion, for the time is come to have mercy on it.

℣. The Lord be with you. ℟. And with thy spirit. ◥

Postcommunion. Grant to us, almighty God, that by the temporal death of Thy Son to which these venerable rites bear witness, we may trust that Thou hast given to us everlasting life. Through the same, etc. ℟. Amen. ◥

Prayer Over The People. Let us pray. Bow down your heads before God.

Look down, we beseech Thee, O Lord, on this Thy family, for which our Lord Jesus Christ did not hesitate to be delivered up into the hands of wicked men, and to suffer the torment of the Cross. Who with Thee, etc. ℟. Amen.

  • *Final Prayers, page 20.*

SOLEMN EVENING MASS OF THE LORD'S SUPPER ON HOLY THURSDAY

Priv. Feria, Dbl. 1st Cl.   White

Station: St. John Lateran

Today Holy Communion may be distributed to the people only during the evening Masses or immediately after them.

The Mass of the Lord's Supper is celebrated in the evening at the most convenient time, but not before 5 P.M. nor after 8 P.M. Visits to repositories are to begin after the Holy Thursday evening Mass and are to last through the night.

The Tabernacle on the main Altar is completely empty. However, in order to allow the Clergy and people to receive Holy Communion today and tomorrow, a pyx (or pyxes) is placed on the Altar, containing hosts to be consecrated in this Mass.

Where there are not enough Clerics and Priests, Mass is celebrated according to the rite for sung Masses, and the incensation of the Altar is permitted as in Solemn Masses.

However, where there are Clerics, it is most fitting that they take part in the Solemn Evening Mass in the regular form of assistance in choir.

Therefore, everyone puts on his choral vestments: Priests add the stole; the Celebrant and Ministers wear the usual Mass vestments in white.

When everyone is ready, the Procession moves through the church to the Altar, while the Choir sings the Introit.

Introit. *Gal. 6, 14.* But it behooves us to glory in the Cross of our Lord Jesus Christ: in Whom is our salvation, life, and resurrection: by Whom we are saved and delivered. *Ps. 66, 2.* May God have mercy on us, and bless us: may He cause the light of His countenance to shine upon us; and may He have mercy on us.—But it behooves.

Arriving at the Altar with his Ministers (or servers), the Celebrant says the prayers at the foot of the Altar, and, ascending, kisses the middle of the Altar. Then he incenses the Altar in the usual manner, even when he celebrates a sung Mass alone.

After incensing the Altar, the Celebrant reads the Introit and recites the Kyrie, page 5. Then he solemnly begins the "Glória in excélsis." The bells are rung and the organ is played through the entire hymn, after which they are silent until the Easter Vigil.

Prayer. O God, from Whom Judas received the punishment of his guilt, and the thief, the reward of his confession, grant unto us the full fruit of Thy clemency, that even as in His Passion, our Lord Jesus Christ gave to each a retribution according to His merits, so, having taken away our past sins, He may bestow on us the grace of His Resurrection. Who with Thee liveth, etc. *S.* Amen. ⸎

Epistle. *1 Cor. 11, 20-32.* Brethren: When you meet together, it is no longer possible to eat the Lord's Supper. For at the meal, each one takes first his own supper, and one is hungry, and another drinks overmuch. Have you not houses for your eating and drinking? Or do you despise the church of God and put to shame the needy? What am I to say to you? Am I to commend you? In this I do not commend you. For I myself have received from the Lord (what I also delivered to you), that the Lord Jesus, on the night in which He was betrayed, took bread, and giving thanks broke, and said, "This is My body which shall be

given up for you; do this in remembrance of Me."
In like manner also the cup, after He had supped,
saying, "This cup is the new covenant in My
blood; do this as often as you drink it, in remembrance of Me. For as often as you shall eat this
bread and drink the cup, you proclaim the death
of the Lord, until He comes." Therefore whoever
eats this bread or drinks the cup of the Lord unworthily, will be guilty of the body and the blood
of the Lord. But let a man prove himself, and so
let him eat of that bread and drink of the cup;
for he who eats and drinks unworthily, without dis-
tinguishing the body, eats and drinks judgment to
himself. This is why many among you are infirm
and weak, and many sleep. But if we judged ourselves, we should not thus be judged. But when
we are judged, we are being chastised by the Lord
that we may not be condemned with this world.
S. Thanks be to God. ⸜

Gradual. *Phil. 2, 8-9.* Christ became obedient
for us unto death, even to death on a Cross. ℣.
Therefore, God also has exalted Him and has
given Him the Name that is above every name.

● *Prayer: Cleanse My Heart, page 6.*

Gospel. *John 13, 1-15.* Before the feast of the
Passover, Jesus, knowing that the hour had come
for Him to pass out of this world to the Father,
having loved His own who were in the world,
loved them to the end. And during the supper, the
devil having already put it into the heart of Judas
Iscariot, the son of Simon, to betray Him, Jesus,
knowing that the Father had given all things into
His hands, and that He had come forth from God
and was going to God, rose from the supper and
laid aside His garments, and taking a towel girded
Himself. Then He poured water into the basin and
began to wash the feet of the disciples, and to dry
them with the towel with which He was girded.
He came, then, to Simon Peter. And Peter said to

Him, "Lord, dost Thou wash my feet?" Jesus answered and said to him, "What I do thou knowest not now; but thou shalt know hereafter." Peter said to Him, "Thou shalt never wash my feet!" Jesus answered him, "If I do not wash thee, thou shalt have no part with Me." Simon Peter said to Him, "Lord, not my feet only, but also my hands and my head!" Jesus said to him, "He who has bathed needs only to wash, and he is clean all over. And you are clean, but not all." For He knew who it was that would betray Him. This is why He said, "You are not all clean." Now after He had washed their feet and put on His garments, when He had reclined again, He said to them, "Do you know what I have done to you? You call Me Master and Lord, and you say well, for so I am. If, therefore, I the Lord and Master have washed your feet, you also ought to wash the feet of one another. For I have given you an example, that as I have done to you, so you also should do." S. Praise be to Thee, O Christ.

It is most fitting that a brief Sermon be given after the Gospel to explain the ineffable Mysteries recalled by this Mass, the institution of the Holy Eucharist and the Priesthood, and our Lord's commandment on fraternal charity.

The Creed is not said.

The Washing of the Feet

After the Sermon, the Washing of the Feet takes place wherever a pastoral reason suggests it.

Seats for twelve men whose feet will be washed are distributed in the sanctuary, or in the church proper. The other things that will be needed, are placed on a small table at the proper time.

In the meantime, the Deacon and Subdeacon (or two of the older servers), lead the twelve men chosen, two by two, to the prepared place, while the Choir, or the assisting Clergy itself, begins singing or reciting the antiphons, psalms and verses given below.

After the proper reverence to the Altar and to the Cele-brant, who is sitting in the sanctuary, the twelve chosen men also sit down. Then the sacred Ministers (or servers) approach the Celebrant. All remove their maniples, and the Celebrant even his chasuble.

When the washing of the feet is about to conclude, the 8th antiphon with its verses is begun. The rest are omitted, if necessary.

The antiphons, psalms and verses to be sung or recited are:

1st Antiphon. *John 13, 34.* "A new command-ment I give you, that you love one another, as I have loved you," saith the Lord. *Ps. 118, 1.* Blessed are the undefiled in the way: who walk in the law of the Lord.

Each antiphon is repeated in full up to the psalm-verse.

2nd Antiphon. *John 13, 4. 5. 15.* After the Lord had risen from supper, He poured water into a basin, and began to wash the feet of His disciples: to whom He gave this example. *Ps. 47, 2.* Great is the Lord, and exceedingly to be praised in the city of our God, in His holy mountain.

Ant. After the Lord, etc.

3rd Antiphon. *John 13, 12. 13. 15.* The Lord Jesus, after He had supped with His disciples, washed their feet, and said to them: "Do you know what I your Lord and Master have done to you? I have given you an example, that so you also should do." *Ps. 84, 2.* Thou hast blessed, O Lord, Thy land; Thou hast turned away the captivity of Jacob.

Ant. The Lord Jesus, etc.

4th Antiphon. *John 13, 6-8.* "Lord, dost Thou wash my feet?" Jesus answered and said to him, "If I do not wash thy feet, thou shalt have no part with Me." ℣. He came to Simon Peter, and Peter said to Him, "Lord, dost Thou wash my feet?"

Jesus answered and said to him, "If I do not wash thy feet, thou shalt have no part with Me." ℣. What I do, thou knowest not now; but thou shalt know hereafter.

Ant. Lord, dost Thou, etc.

5th Antiphon. If I, your Lord and Master, have washed your feet, how much more ought you to wash one another's feet? *Ps. 48, 2.* Hear these things, all you nations: give ear, you who inhabit the world.

Ant. If I, your Lord, etc.

6th Antiphon. *John 13, 35.* By this shall all men know that you are My disciples, if you have love for one another. ℣. Jesus said to His disciples.

Ant. By this shall, etc.

7th Antiphon. *1 Cor. 13, 13.* Let these three, faith, hope and charity abide in you; but the greatest of these is charity. ℣. And now there remain faith, hope and charity, these three; but the greatest of these is charity.

Ant. Let these three, etc.

The following antiphon with its versicles is never omitted; but, if the Washing of the Feet is nearing the end, the following antiphon is begun, and, if necessary, the preceding ones are omitted.

8th Antiphon. Where charity and love are, there is God. ℣. The love of Christ has gathered us together. ℣. Let us rejoice in Him and be glad. ℣. Let us fear and love the living God. ℣. And let us love one another with a sincere heart.

Ant. Where charity and love are, there is God.

℣. When, therefore, we are assembled together. ℣. Let us take heed, that we be not divided in mind. ℣. Let malicious quarrels and contentions cease. ℣. And let Christ our God dwell among us.

Ant. Where charity and love are, there is God.

℣. Let us also with the blessed see. ℣. Thy face in glory, O Christ our God. ℣. There to possess immeasurable and happy joy. ℣. For infinite ages of ages. Amen.

In the meantime, the Celebrant proceeds to the Washing of the Feet in this manner: He girds himself with a towel and then begins to wash, in order, the feet of those who have been chosen for the washing. The Acolytes provide the basin and water, the Subdeacon holds the right foot of each person, and the Celebrant, kneeling before each, washes his foot and dries it with the towel provided by the Deacon.

(When there are no Deacon and Subdeacon, the functions performed by them in a Solemn Mass, are carried out by the servers.)

After the Washing of the Feet, the Celebrant washes and dries his hands silently. Then all put on the maniple, the Celebrant adding also the chasuble, and return to the middle of the Altar, where the Celebrant says:

Our Father, etc. *(silently)*.

℣. And lead us not into temptation. ℟. But deliver us from evil.

℣. Thou hast commanded Thy commandments, O Lord. ℟. To be exactly observed.

℣. Thou hast washed the feet of Thy disciples. ℟. Despise not the work of Thy hands.

℣. O Lord, hear my prayer. ℟. And let my cry come unto Thee.

℣. The Lord be with you. ℟. And with thy spirit.

Let us pray. Be present, O Lord, we beseech Thee, at the performance of our service: and since Thou didst vouchsafe to wash the feet of Thy disciples, despise not the work of Thy hands, which Thou hast commanded us to perpetuate, that, as here the outward stains are washed away by us and for us, so the inward sins of us all may be blotted out by Thee. Which do Thou deign to grant, Who livest and reignest God, world without end. Amen.

At the end of the prayer, the twelve men make the proper reverence to the Altar and to the Celebrant, and return to their places—to the sanctuary if they are Clerics, or to their designated place if they are lay people.

However, where the Washing of the Feet must be held outside of Mass, the rite described above is to be observed with one addition. The Gospel of the Mass, "Before the feast," page 62, is first sung in the usual manner.

After the Washing of the Feet, or, when this does not take place, after the Sermon, the Mass is continued as usual.

P. The Lord be with you. S. And with thy spirit. ⟩

Offertory. *Ps. 117, 16. 17.* The right hand of the Lord has wrought strength: the right hand of the Lord has exalted me. I shall not die, but live, and shall declare the works of the Lord.

• *Offertory Prayers, page 8.*

Secret. We beseech Thee, O holy Lord, Father almighty, everlasting God, that He Himself may render our sacrifice acceptable to Thee, Who, bv the tradition of today, taught His disciples to do this in commemoration of Him, Jesus Christ, Thy Son our Lord. Who with Thee, etc.

• *Preface of the Holy Cross, page 11.*

• *Canon, page 12, up to "Commemoration of the Saints."*

Commemoration of the Saints

In the unity of holy fellowship, we honor the most sacred day on which our Lord Jesus Christ was betrayed for us; and we also observe the memory, first of all, of the glorious and ever Virgin Mary, Mother of our Lord and God Jesus Christ; next that of Thy Blessed Apostles and Martyrs, Peter and Paul, Andrew, James, John, Thomas, James, Philip, Bartholomew, Matthew, Simon and Thaddeus; of Linus, Cletus, Clement, Sixtus, Cornelius, Cyprian, Lawrence, Chrysogonus. John and Paul, Cosmas and Damian, and of all Thy Saints, by whose merits and prayers grant that we may be always fortified by the help of Thy protection. (*He joins his hands.*) Through the same Christ our Lord. Amen.

Holding his hands outstretched over the offering, he says:

Graciously accept, then, we beseech Thee, O Lord, this service of our worship and that of all Thy household, which we offer to Thee in memory of the day on which our Lord Jesus Christ gave to His disciples the mysteries of His Body and Blood to be celebrated. Order our days in Thy peace, save us from everlasting damnation, and cause us to be numbered among Thy chosen ones. (*He joins his hands.*) Through the same Christ our Lord. Amen.

Do Thou, O God, deign (*He makes the Sign of the Cross three times over the offering*) to bless ✠ what we offer, and make it approved, ✠ effective, ✠ right, and wholly pleasing in every way, that it may become (*He makes the Sign of the Cross over the host*) for our good, the Body ✠ (*and over the chalice*) and Blood ✠ of Thy dearly beloved Son, (*He joins his hands*) Jesus Christ our Lord.

Today the incensation of the Blessed Sacrament, as in Solemn Masses, takes place even if the Mass is celebrated without Ministers. In this case, it is performed by the Acolytes (or servers).

Who, on the day before He suffered for our salvation and that of all men, that is, this day (*He takes the host*), took bread into His holy and venerable hands (*Raises his eyes to heaven*), and having raised His eyes to heaven, unto Thee, O God, His Almighty Father (*Bows his head*), giving thanks to Thee (*Makes the Sign of the Cross over the host*), He ✠ blessed it, broke it, and gave it to His disciples, saying, "Take and eat ye all of this:

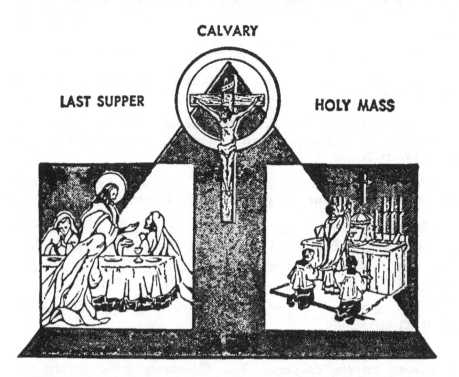

CALVARY

LAST SUPPER

HOLY MASS

Holding the host between the thumbs and index fingers of both hands, he says the words of consecration secretly, distinctly and attentively over the host, and at the same time over all the hosts if more are to be consecrated.

FOR THIS IS MY BODY.

In like manner, when the supper was done, taking also this goodly chalice into His holy and venerable hands, again giving thanks to Thee, He blessed ✠ it, and gave it to His disciples, saying: Take ye all, and drink of this:

FOR THIS IS THE CHALICE OF MY BLOOD OF THE NEW AND ETERNAL COVENANT; THE MYSTERY OF FAITH, WHICH SHALL BE SHED FOR YOU AND FOR MANY UNTO THE FORGIVENESS OF SINS.

He then replaces the chalice on the corporal, and says:

As often as you shall do these things, in memory of Me shall you do them.

The remainder of the Canon, page 14, "Mindful, therefore," etc.

The Kiss of Peace is not given, and the prayer, "O Lord Jesus, Who hast said," page 17, is omitted.

After receiving the Precious Blood, the Celebrant administers Holy Communion as usual, the Confiteor and absolution being omitted.

The Communion antiphon may be sung by the Choir while the Celebrant distributes Holy Communion.

Communion. *John 13, 12. 13. 15.* The Lord Jesus, after He had supped with His disciples, washed their feet, and said to them, "Do you know what I, your Lord and Master, have done to you? I have given you an example, that so you also should do."

After the Communion of the Faithful, the pyx (or pyxes) is placed on the corporal. The Celebrant proceeds to the purification of the chalice and his fingers, saying the usual prayers, page 20.

The Mass continues as usual, except that the Celebrant genuflects whenever he comes to or departs from the middle of the Altar, or passes before the Blessed Sacrament; and when he says "The Lord be with you," he does not turn to the people at the middle of the Altar but at the Gospel side, so that he does not turn his back to the Blessed Sacrament.

℣. The Lord be with you. ℟. And with thy spirit.

Postcommunion. Strengthened with life-giving food, we beseech Thee, O Lord, our God, that what we do during our mortal life, may bring us to the reward of life immortal with Thee. Through our Lord, etc. ℟. Amen.

In place of "Go, you are dismissed," page 20, today is sung "Let us bless the Lord," and the prayer "May the tribute," page 20, is said as usual.

The Blessing and the Last Gospel, page 21, are omitted. Instead the Celebrant takes off the maniple (the Ministers do likewise) and the chasuble, and puts on a white cope.

Low Masses, which may be permitted by the local Ordinary, are terminated in the usual manner.

The Solemn Transferal and Reservation of the Blessed Sacrament and the Stripping of the Altars

Immediately after Mass, there occurs the solemn Transferal and Reservation of the Blessed Sacrament, which is kept in a pyx to be given in Holy Communion tomorrow.

The procedure for the Transferal and Reservation is as follows: torches are lighted and the Procession takes place.

Standing at the foot of the Altar, the Celebrant places incense in two thuribles but does not bless it. Then, kneeling, he incenses the Blessed Sacrament three times.

Next he puts on a white humeral veil and ascends the Altar. Genuflecting at the middle of the Altar, he rises, takes the pyx from the Deacon and covers it with the ends of the veil.

Then he descends from the Altar and, walking under the baldachinum, he proceeds to the place prepared for the reservation while two Acolytes (or servers) continuously incense the Blessed Sacrament.

During the Procession, the following hymn is sung:

Pange Lingua

Sing my tongue, the Savior's glory,
Of His Flesh the mystery sing;
Of His Blood all price exceeding,
Shed by our immortal King,
Destined for the world's redemption,
From a noble womb to spring.

Of a pure and spotless Virgin,
Born for us on earth below,
He, as Man with man conversing,
Stayed the seeds of truth to sow
Then He closed in solemn order
Wondrously His life of woe.

On the night of that Last Supper,
Seated with His chosen band,
He, the Paschal Victim eating,
First fulfills the Law's command;
Then as food to all His brethren
Gives Himself with His own Hand.

Word made Flesh, the bread of nature,
By His word to Flesh He turns;
Wine into His Blood He changes:
What though sense no change discerns,
Only be the heart in earnest,
Faith her lesson quickly learns.

Arriving at the Repository, the Celebrant places the pyx on the Altar (aided by the Deacon if necessary), kneels and incenses the Blessed Sacrament after again putting incense into the thurible. Here the "Tantum ergo" is sung:

Down in adoration falling,
Lo! the sacred Host we hail,
Lo! o'er ancient forms departing
Newer rites of grace prevail;
Faith for all defects supplying,
Where the feeble senses fail.

To the everlasting Father,
And the Son Who reigns on high
With the Holy Ghost proceeding
Forth from each eternally,
Be salvation, honor, blessing,
Might and endless majesty. Amen.

Then the Deacon (or the Celebrant himself) places the pyx in the Tabernacle or Repository.

Afterwards all kneel and silently adore the Blessed Sacrament for a period of time. At a given signal, the Celebrant and Ministers (and servers) rise, again adore the Blessed Sacrament on both knees, and return to the sacristy. The Celebrant and Ministers remove the white vestments, and the Celebrant and Deacon put on purple stoles.

However, if there are several pyxes to be transferred, the Celebrant himself (or, if present, another Priest or Deacon, wearing surplice, white stole and humeral veil) brings them to the appointed place before the Stripping of the Altars begins. This transferal takes place simply: two Acolytes (or servers) carry lighted candles and another carries the ombrellino.

Then the Celebrant goes to the main Altar with his Ministers; after bowing to the Altar, standing, they begin the Stripping of the Altars as follows:

The Celebrant says the antiphon below in a loud voice and then begins the first verse of Psalm 21 as far as the words "forsaken me."

If there are Clerics present, they continue the recitation of this psalm until the Stripping of the Altars is completed; if not, the Celebrant himself continues the psalm.

Meanwhile the Celebrant and his Ministers (or servers) strip all the Altars of the church, except the one where the Blessed Sacrament is solemnly adored.

After they have finished, they come back to the main Altar, the Celebrant repeats the antiphon, and they return to the sacristy.

Ant. They parted my garments amongst them. and upon my vesture they cast lots.

Psalm 21. My God, my God, look upon me: why hast Thou forsaken me? Far from my salvation are the words of my sins. O my God, I shall cry by day, and Thou wilt not hear: and by night, and it shall not be reputed as folly in me. But Thou dwellest in the holy place, the praise of Israel. In Thee have our fathers hoped: they have hoped, and Thou hast delivered them. They cried to Thee, and they were saved: they trusted in Thee, and were not confounded.

But I am a worm and no man: the reproach of men, and the outcast of the people. All they who saw me have laughed me to scorn: they have spoken with the lips, and wagged the head. He hoped in the Lord, let Him deliver him: let Him save him, seeing he delights in Him. For Thou art He Who hast drawn me out of the womb: my hope from the breasts of my mother. I was cast upon Thee from the womb. From my mother's womb Thou art my God: depart not from me.

For tribulation is very near; for there is none to help me. Many calves have surrounded me: fat bulls have besieged me. They have opened their mouths against me as a lion ravening and roaring.

I am poured out like water, and all my bones are scattered. My heart is become like wax melting in the midst of my bowels. My strength is dried up like a potsherd, and my tongue has cleaved to my jaws; and Thou hast brought me down into the dust of death.

For many dogs have encompassed me: the council of the malignant has besieged me. They have pierced my hands and my feet: they have numbered all my bones. They have looked and stared upon me. They parted my garments among them, and upon my vesture they cast lots.

But Thou, O Lord, remove not Thy help to a distance from me: look toward my defense. O God, deliver my soul from the sword: my only one from the hand of the dog! Save me from the lion's mouth; and my lowness from the horns of the unicorns.

I will declare Thy name to my brethren: in the midst of the church will I praise Thee. You who fear the Lord, praise Him: all you seed of Jacob, glorify Him. Let all the seed of Israel fear Him: because He has not slighted nor despised the supplication of the poor man. Neither has He turned away His face from me: but when I cried to Him, He heard me. With Thee is my praise in a great church: I will pay my vows in the sight of those who fear Him. The poor shall eat and shall be filled, and they shall praise the Lord who seek Him: their hearts shall live forever and ever.

All the ends of the earth shall remember and shall be converted to the Lord. And all the kindreds of the Gentiles shall adore in His sight. For the kingdom is the Lord's: and He shall have dominion over the nations. All the fat ones of the earth have eaten and have adored: all they who go down to the earth shall fall before Him. And to Him my soul shall live: and my seed shall serve Him. There shall be declared to the Lord a generation to come: and the heavens shall show forth His justice to a people that shall be born, which the Lord has made.

Ant. They parted, etc., page 73.

"Not a bone of Him shall you break."

THE SOLEMN LITURGICAL AFTERNOON SERVICE OF OUR LORD'S PASSION AND DEATH ON GOOD FRIDAY

Priv. Feria, Dbl. 1st Cl.   Black and Purple

Station: Holy Cross in Jerusalem

Holy Communion may be distributed only at the solemn liturgical service in the afternoon, except to the sick and to those in danger of death.

The following services must be held between three and six o'clock in the afternoon. *("Instruction on the Correct Use of the Restored Ordo of Holy Week," Nov. 16, 1955.)*

1st Part of the Liturgical Service—The Readings

The Altar is completely stripped: without cross, without candelabra, and without Altar cloths.

Today's solemn liturgical service, which takes place in the afternoon, is accomplished by a Celebrant with the assistance of servers where there is not a sufficient number of Clerics and Priests, as will be noted below. Where there are Clerics, it is preferable that they assist at the liturgical service in choir.

Accordingly, each one vests in his own choir vestments; the Celebrant and Deacon, with amice, alb, cincture, and black stole; the Subdeacon, with amice, alb and cincture.

When all have been vested, the Procession proceeds through the church to the Altar in silence.

When the Clerics, Ministers (or servers) and Celebrant reach the Altar, they make the proper reverence; then, the

Celebrant and sacred Ministers (not the servers) prostrate themselves face downwards, and the rest go to their benches in the sanctuary (or choir) and remain there kneeling in a profound bow: all pray for some time in silence.

At a given signal all raise themselves but remain kneeling; only the Celebrant, standing before the steps of the Altar with joined hands, says the following prayer in a ferial tone:

Prayer. O God, Who, by the Passion of Christ, our Lord, hast destroyed the hereditary death of the ancient sin, to which humankind had succumbed: grant that we may be made like to Him and, just as by necessity we have borne the image of an earthly nature, so by sanctification we may also bear the image of heavenly grace. Through the same Christ our Lord. *All respond*: Amen.

At the end of the prayer the Celebrant and Ministers (or servers) go to the bench. Meanwhile an unadorned lectern is placed in the middle of the sanctuary and a Lector begins the first Lesson, while all are seated directing their attention to him.

1st Lesson. *Osee 6, 1-6.* Thus saith the Lord: In their affliction they will rise early to Me: Come, and let us return to the Lord, for He has taken us, and He will heal us, He will strike, and He will cure us. He will revive us after two days: on the third day He will raise us up and we shall live in His sight. We shall know and we shall follow on, that we may know the Lord. His going forth is prepared as the morning light and He will come to us as the early and the latter rain to the earth. What shall I do to Thee, O Ephraim? What shall I do to thee, O Juda? Your mercy is as a morning cloud and as the dew that goes away in the morning. For this reason have I hewed them by the Prophets, I have slain them by the words of my mouth: and thy judgments shall go forth as the light. For I desired mercy and not sacrifice: and the knowledge of God more than holocausts.

The following Responsory is sung by the Choir or is read by an assistant Cleric.

Responsory. *Hab. 3.* O Lord, I have heard Thy hearing and was afraid: I have considered Thy works and trembled. ℣. In the midst of two animals Thou shalt be made known: when the years shall draw near Thou shalt be known: when the time shall come, Thou shalt be manifested. ℣. When my soul shall be in trouble, Thou wilt remember mercy, even in Thy wrath. ℣. God will come from Libanus, and the Holy One from the shady and thickly covered mountain. ℣. His majesty covered the heavens: and the earth is full of His praise.

At the end of the Responsory, all rise; the Celebrant, standing at the bench says: "Let us pray"; the Deacon: "Let us kneel," and all kneel down for some time and pray silently; when the Deacon says: "Arise," all rise, and the Celebrant with hands joined and in a ferial tone says the prayer.

(When there are no Deacon and Subdeacon, the Celebrant remains in his own place, says: "Let us pray," "Let us kneel," and after a short silent prayer on his knees, he says: "Arise." Then he rises and with joined hands and in a ferial tone says the prayer.)

Let us pray. ℣. Let us kneel. ℟. Arise.

Prayer. O God, from Whom Judas received the punishment of his guilt, and the thief, the reward of his confession, grant unto us the full fruit of Thy clemency, that even as in His Passion, our Lord Jesus Christ gave to each a retribution according to His merits, so, having taken away our past sins, He may bestow on us the grace of His Resurrection. Who with Thee, etc. ℟. Amen.

At the end of the prayer, the next Lesson is said at the lectern by the Subdeacon. The Celebrant and all others are seated and direct their attention to him.

2nd Lesson. *Ex. 12, 1-11.* In those days, the Lord said to Moses and Aaron in the land of Egypt: This month shall be to you the beginning of months: it shall be the first in the months of the year. Speak ye to the whole assembly of the children of Israel, and say to them: On the tenth day of this month let every man take a lamb by their families and houses. But if the number be less than may suffice to eat the lamb, he shall take unto him his neighbor who joins to his house, according to the number of souls which may be enough to eat the lamb. And it shall be a lamb without blemish, a male, of one year: according to which rite also you shall take a kid. And you shall keep it until the fourteenth day of this month: and the whole multitude of the children of Israel shall sacrifice it in the evening. And they shall take of the blood thereof, and put it upon both the side posts, and on the upper door posts of the houses, wherein they shall eat it. And they shall eat the flesh that night roasted at the fire: and unleavened bread with wild lettuce. You shall not eat thereof anything raw, nor boiled in water, but only roasted at the fire. You shall eat the head with the feet and entrails thereof. Neither shall there remain anything of it until morning. If there be anything left, you shall burn it with fire. And thus you shall eat it: You shall gird your reins, and you shall have shoes on your feet, holding staves in your hands, and you shall eat in haste; for it is the Phase (that is, the Passage) of the Lord.

The following Responsory is sung by the Choir or is read by an assistant Cleric.

Responsory. *Ps. 139, 2-10. 14.* Deliver me, O Lord, from the evil man: rescue me from the unjust man. ℣. Who have devised iniquities in their hearts: all the day long they designed battles. ℣. They have sharpened their tongues like a serpent; the venom of asps is under their lips. ℣. Keep me, O Lord, from the hand of the wicked: and from unjust men deliver me. ℣. Who have proposed to supplant my steps. The proud have hidden a net for me. ℣. And they have stretched out cords for a snare for my feet; they have laid for me a stumbling-block by the wayside. ℣. I said to the Lord: Thou art my God. Hear, O Lord, the voice of my supplication. ℣. O Lord, Lord, the strength of my salvation: overshadow my head in the day of battle. ℣. Give me not up from my desire to the wicked: they have plotted against me. Do not Thou forsake me, lest at any time they should triumph. ℣. The head of them compassing me about: the labor of their lips shall overwhelm them. ℣. But the just shall give glory to Thy name: and the upright shall dwell with Thy countenance.

At the end of the 2nd Lesson with its Responsory, unadorned lecterns are placed on the floor of the Gospel side of the sanctuary with books, and the singing or reading of the history of the Lord's Passion according to St. John begins in the following manner: It must be sung or read by Ministers who are ordained Deacons.

Assisted by two Acolytes (or servers), without candles or incense, and having made the proper reverence before the Altar, three Deacons stand before the Celebrant. As they bow low, the Celebrant, in a clear voice, says over them:

The Lord be in your hearts and on your lips.

They then stand erect and say: "Amen."

Then again making the proper reverence to the Altar, they go to the Gospel side, where, at uncovered lecterns, they begin to sing or read the history of the Lord's Passion, while all direct their attention to them.

(When there are no Deacon and Subdeacon, the Celebrant sings or reads the history of the Lord's Passion clearly and distinctly. Before he begins, bowing low in the middle of the sanctuary, he says in a clear voice: "The Lord be in my heart and on my lips. Amen." Then, after making the proper reverence before the Altar, he goes to the Gospel side, where, standing before an unadorned lectern, he begins to sing or read the history of the Lord's Passion.)

PASSION OF OUR LORD JESUS CHRIST
John 18, 1-40; 19, 1-42

A T THAT time, Jesus went forth with His disciples beyond the torrent of Cedron, where

there was a garden into which He and His disciples entered. Now Judas, who betrayed Him, also
knew the place, since Jesus had often met there
together with His disciples. Judas, then, taking the
cohort, and attendants from the chief priests and
Pharisees, came there with lanterns, and torches,
and weapons. Jesus therefore knowing all that was
to come upon Him, went forth and said to them,
"Whom do you seek?" They answered Him, "Jesus
of Nazareth." Jesus said to them, "I am He." Now
Judas, who betrayed Him, was also standing with
them. When, therefore, He said to them, "I am
He," they drew back and fell to the ground. So
He asked them again, "Whom do you seek?" And
they said, "Jesus of Nazareth." Jesus answered, "I
have told you that I am He. If, therefore, you seek
Me, let these go their way." That the word which
He said might be fulfilled, "Of those whom Thou
hast given Me, I have not lost one."

Simon Peter therefore, having a sword, drew it
and struck the servant of the high priest and cut
off his right ear. Now the servant's name was Mal-
chus. Jesus therefore said to Peter, "Put up thy
sword into the scabbard. Shall I not drink the cup
that the Father has given Me?" The cohort therefore and the tribune and the attendants of the
Jews seized Jesus and bound Him.

And they brought Him to Annas first, for he
was the father-in-law of Caiphas, who was the
high priest that year. Now it was Caiphas who had
given the counsel to the Jews that it was expedi-
ent that one man should die for the people. But
Simon Peter was following Jesus, and so was another disciple. Now that disciple was known to the
high priest, and he entered with Jesus into the
courtyard of the high priest.

But Peter was standing outside at the gate. So
the other disciple, who was known to the high
priest, went out and spoke to the portress, and

brought Peter in. The maid, who was portress, said therefore to Peter, "Art thou also one of this Man's disciples?" He said, "I am not." Now the servants and attendants were standing at a coal fire and warming themselves, for it was cold. And Peter also was with them, standing and warming himself.

The high priest therefore questioned Jesus concerning His disciples, and concerning His teaching. Jesus answered him, "I have spoken openly to the world; I have always taught in the synagogue and in the temple, where all the Jews gather, and in secret I have said nothing. Why dost thou question Me? Question those who have heard what I spoke to them; behold, these know what I have said." Now when He had said these things, one of the attendants who was standing by struck Jesus a blow, saying, "Is that the way Thou dost answer the high priest?" Jesus answered him, "If I have spoken ill, bear witness to the evil; but if well, why dost thou strike Me?"

And Annas sent Him bound to Caiphas, the high priest. But Simon Peter was standing and warming himself. They therefore said to him, "Art thou also one of His disciples?" He denied it, and said, "I am not." One of the servants of the high priest, a relative of him whose ear Peter had cut off, said, "Did I not see thee in the garden with Him?" Again, therefore, Peter denied it; and at that moment a cock crowed.

They therefore led Jesus from Caiphas to the prætorium. Now it was early morning, and they themselves did not enter the prætorium, that they might not be defiled, but might eat the passover. Pilate therefore went outside to them, and said, "What accusation do you bring against this Man?" They said to him in answer, "If He were not a criminal we should not have handed Him over to thee." Pilate therefore said to them, "Take Him yourselves, and judge Him according to your law."

The Jews, then, said to him, "It is not lawful for us to put anyone to death." This was in fulfillment of what Jesus had said, indicating the manner of His death.

Pilate therefore again entered into the prætorium, and he summoned Jesus, and said to Him, "Art Thou the king of the Jews?" Jesus answered, "Dost thou say this of thyself, or have others told thee of Me?" Pilate answered, "Am I a Jew? Thy own people and the chief priests have delivered Thee to me. What hast Thou done?" Jesus answered, "My kingdom is not of this world. If My kingdom were of this world, My followers would have fought that I might not be delivered to the Jews. But, as it is, My kingdom is not from here." Pilate therefore said to Him, "Thou art then a king?" Jesus answered, "Thou sayest it; I am a king. This is why I was born, and why I have come into the world, to bear witness to the truth. Everyone who is of the truth hears My voice." Pilate said to Him. "What is truth?" And when he had said this, he went outside to the Jews again, and said to them, "I find no guilt in Him. But you have a custom that I should release someone to you at the Passover. Do you wish, therefore, that I release to you the king of the Jews?" They all therefore cried out again, "Not this man, but Barabbas!" Now Barabbas was a robber.

Pilate, then, took Jesus and had Him scourged. And the soldiers, plaiting a crown of thorns, put it upon His head, and arrayed Him in a purple cloak. And they kept coming to Him and saying, "Hail, King of the Jews!" and striking Him.

Pilate therefore again went outside and said to them, "Behold, I bring Him out to you, that you may know that I find no guilt in Him." Jesus therefore came forth, wearing the crown of thorns and the purple cloak. And he said to them "Behold, the Man!" When, therefore, the chief priests and the attendants saw Him, they cried out, saying, "Crucify Him! Crucify Him!" Pilate said to them, "Take Him yourselves and crucify Him, for I find no guilt in Him." The Jews answered him, "We have a Law, and according to that Law He must die, because He has made Himself Son of God." Now when Pilate heard this statement, he feared the more.

And he again went back into the prætorium, and said to Jesus, "Where art Thou from?" But Jesus gave him no answer. Pilate therefore said to Him, "Dost Thou not speak to me? Dost Thou not know that I have power to crucify Thee, and that I have power to release Thee?" Jesus answered, "Thou wouldst have no power at all over Me were it not given thee from above. Therefore, he who betrayed Me to thee has the greater sin." And from then on Pilate was looking for a way to release Him. But the Jews cried out, saying, "If thou release this man, thou art no friend of Cæsar; for everyone who makes himself king sets himself against Cæsar." Pilate therefore, when he heard these words, brought Jesus outside, and sat down on the judgment-seat, at a place called Lithostrotos, but in Hebrew, Gabbatha. Now it was the Preparation Day for the Passover, about the sixth hour. And he said to the Jews, "Behold, your King!" But they cried out, "Away with Him! Away with Him! Crucify Him!" Pilate said to them, "Shall I crucify your King?" The chief priests answered, "We have no king but Cæsar." Then he handed Him over to them to be crucified.

And so they took Jesus and led Him away. And bearing the Cross for Himself, He went forth to the place called the Skull, in Hebrew, Golgotha, where they crucified Him, and with Him two others, one on each side and Jesus in the center.

And Pilate also wrote an inscription and had it put on the Cross. And there was written, "Jesus of Nazareth, the King of the Jews." Many of the

Jews therefore read this inscription, because the place where Jesus was crucified was near the city; and it was written in Hebrew, in Greek and in Latin. The chief priests of the Jews said therefore to Pilate, "Do not write, 'The King of the Jews,' but, 'He said, I am the King of the Jews.'" Pilate answered, "What I have written, I have written."

The soldiers therefore, when they had crucified Him, took His garments and made of them four parts, to each soldier a part, and also the tunic. Now the tunic was without seam, woven in one piece from the top. They therefore said to one another, "Let us not tear it, but let us cast lots for it, to see whose it shall be." That the Scripture might be fulfilled which says, "They divided My garments among them; and for My vesture they cast lots." These things therefore the soldiers did.

Now there were standing by the Cross of Jesus His mother and His mother's sister, Mary of Cleophas, and Mary Magdalene. When Jesus, therefore, saw His mother and the disciple standing by, whom He loved, He said to His mother, "Woman, behold, thy son." Then He said to the disciple, "Behold, thy mother." And from that hour the disciple took her into his home.

After this Jesus, knowing that all things were now accomplished, that the Scripture might be fulfilled, said, "I thirst." Now there was standing there a vessel full of common wine; and having put a sponge soaked with the wine on a stalk of hyssop, they put it to His mouth. Therefore, when Jesus had taken the wine, He said, "It is consummated!" And bowing His head, He gave up His spirit. *(Here all kneel and pause for a few moments.)*

The Jews therefore, since it was the Preparation Day, in order that the bodies might not remain upon the cross on the Sabbath (for that Sabbath was a solemn day), besought Pilate that their legs might be broken, and that they might be taken away. The soldiers therefore came and broke the legs of the first, and of the other, who had been crucified with Him. But when they came to Jesus, and saw that He was already dead, they did not break His legs; but one of the soldiers opened His side with a lance, and immediately there came out blood and water. And he who saw it has borne witness, and his witness is true; and he knows that he tells the truth, that you also may believe. For these things came to pass that the Scripture might be fulfilled, "Not a bone of Him shall you break." And again another Scripture says, "They shall look upon Him Whom they have pierced."

Now after these things Joseph of Arimathea, because he was a disciple of Jesus (although for fear of the Jews a secret one), besought Pilate that he might take away the body of Jesus. And Pilate gave permission. He came, therefore, and took away the body of Jesus. And there also came Nicodemus (who at first had come to Jesus by night), bringing a mixture of myrrh and aloes, in weight about a hundred pounds. They therefore took the body of Jesus and wrapped it in linen cloths with the spices, after the Jewish manner of preparing for burial. Now in the place where He was crucified there was a garden, and in the garden a new tomb in which no one had yet been laid. There, accordingly, because of the Preparation Day of the Jews, for the tomb was close at hand, they laid Jesus. S. Praise be to Thee, O Christ.

2nd Part of the Liturgical Service—The Solemn Prayers Also Called "The Prayer of the Faithful"

After the history of the Lord's Passion is finished, the Celebrant puts on a black cope; the Deacon and Subdeacon put on the dalmatic or tunicle of the same color.

In the meantime two Acolytes (or servers) spread only one altar cloth on the Altar, and place the Missal in the center.

Then the Celebrant, assisted by Ministers (or servers) goes to the Altar, ascends and kisses the middle of the Altar. He stands there before the Missal and begins the solemn prayers, while the Ministers stand on each side of him.

The beginning of each of the following prayers expresses their particular intentions. The prefaces are sung by the Celebrant with hands joined; then the Celebrant says: "Let us pray," the Deacon says: "Let us kneel," and all kneel down for some time in silent prayer; when the Deacon says: "Arise," all rise, and the Celebrant with extended hands and in a ferial tone says the prayer.

(When there are no Deacon and Subdeacon, the Celebrant says: "Let us pray," "Let us kneel," and after kneeling a short time in silent prayer, he says: "Arise"; then he rises and, with extended hands and in a ferial tone says the prayer.)

1. For the Holy Church

Let us pray, dearly beloved, for the holy Church of God, that our Lord and God may deign to give it peace, keep it in unity, and protect it throughout the world, subjecting principalities and powers to it, and may grant unto us that, leading a peaceful and quiet life, we may glorify God, the Father almighty.

Let us pray. ℣. *Let us kneel.* ℟. *Arise.*

Almighty and everlasting God, Who in Christ hast revealed Thy glory to all nations, guard the works of Thy mercy; that Thy Church, spread over the whole world, may with constant faith persevere in the confession of Thy name. Through the same, etc. *All respond:* Amen.

2. For the Supreme Pontiff

Let us pray also for our most Holy Father Pope N., that our Lord and God, Who chose him for the order of the Episcopate, may keep him in health and safety for the good of His holy Church, to govern God's holy people.

Let us pray. ℣. *Let us kneel.* ℟. *Arise.*

Almighty and everlasting God, by Whose judgment all things are established, mercifully regard our prayers, and in Thy goodness preserve the Bishop chosen for us, that the Christian people who are ruled by Thy authority, may under so great a Pontiff be increased in the merits of their faith. Through our Lord, etc. *All respond*: Amen.

3. For All Orders and Degrees of the Faithful

Let us pray also for all Bishops, Priests, Deacons, Subdeacons, Acolytes, Exorcists, Readers, Porters, Confessors, Virgins, Widows, and for all the holy people of God.

Let us pray. ℣. Let us kneel. ℟. Arise.

Almighty and everlasting God, by Whose Spirit the whole body of the Church is sanctified and ruled, hear our humble pleading for all its orders, that by the gift of Thy grace Thou mayest be faithfully served by all degrees. Through our Lord, etc. *All respond*: Amen.

4. For Civil Authorities

Let us pray also for all civil authorities, in the exercise of their ministry and power, that God, our Lord, may direct their minds and hearts in accordance with His will for our everlasting peace.

Let us pray. ℣. Let us kneel. ℟. Arise.

Almighty and everlasting God, Who dost direct the powers and laws of all nations, mercifully regard those who rule over us; that, by Thy protecting right hand, the integrity of religion and the security of each country might prevail everywhere on earth. Through our Lord, etc. *All respond*: Amen.

5. For Catechumens

Let us pray also for our Catechumens, that our Lord and God would open the ears of their hearts, and the gate of mercy; that, having received, by the font of regeneration the remission of all their sins, they also may be found in Christ Jesus our Lord.

Let us pray. ℣. Let us kneel. ℟. Arise.

Almighty and everlasting God, Who dost ever make Thy Church fruitful with new offspring, increase the faith and understanding of our Catechumens; that being born again in the font of Baptism, they may be associated with the children of Thy adoption. Through our Lord, etc. *All respond*: Amen.

6. For the Needs of the Faithful

Let us pray, dearly beloved, to God the Father almighty, that He cleanse the world of all errors: take away diseases, drive away famine, open prisons, break chains, grant a sure return to travellers, health to the sick, and a safe haven to those at sea.

Let us pray. ℣. Let us kneel. ℟. Arise.

Almighty and everlasting God, the comfort of the sorrowful, and the strength of those who labor, let the prayers of those who call upon Thee in any trouble reach Thee; that all may rejoice because in their necessities Thy mercy has helped them. Through our Lord, etc. *All respond*: Amen.

7. For the Unity of the Church

Let us pray also for heretics and schismatics: that our Lord and God may be pleased to deliver them from all their errors, and to recall them to our holy Mother the Catholic and Apostolic Church.

Let us pray. ℣. Let us kneel. ℟. Arise.

Almighty and everlasting God, Who savest all, and willest that no one should perish, look on the souls that are led astray by the deceit of the devil, that having set aside all heretical evil, the hearts of those who err may repent, and return to the unity of Thy truth. Through our Lord, etc. *All respond*: Amen.

8. For the Conversion of the Jews

Let us pray also for the unfaithful Jews, that our God and Lord may remove the veil from their hearts; that they also may acknowledge our Lord Jesus Christ.

Let us pray. ℣. Let us kneel. ℟. Arise.

Almighty and everlasting God, Who drivest not even the faithless Jews away from Thy mercy, hear our prayers, which we offer for the blindness of that people, that, acknowledging the light of Thy truth, which is Christ, they may be rescued from their darkness. Through the same, etc. *All respond*: Amen.

9. For the Conversion of Pagans

Let us pray also for the pagans, that almighty God may remove iniquity from their hearts, that, putting aside their idols, they may be converted to the true and living God, and His only Son, Jesus Christ our God and Lord.

Let us pray. ℣. Let us kneel. ℟. Arise.

Almighty and everlasting God, Who always seekest not the death, but the life of sinners, mercifully hear our prayer, and deliver them from the worship of idols, and join them to Thy holy Church for the praise and glory of Thy name. Through our Lord, etc. *All respond*: Amen.

3rd Part of the Liturgical Service—Solemn Adoration of the Holy Cross

At the end of these prayers, the Celebrant and Ministers return to the bench where the Celebrant removes the cope, the Ministers the dalmatic or tunicle, and the adoration of the Holy Cross begins.

A sufficiently large Cross with Corpus should be used, covered with a purple cloth that can easily be removed.

The Celebrant and Subdeacon remain standing at the bench. The Deacon with the Acolytes (or servers) goes to the sacristy, from which he carries the Cross in procession to the church: the Acolytes (or servers) lead, followed by the Deacon with the Cross, who is flanked by two other Acolytes (or servers) carrying lighted candles.

When they return to the sanctuary, the Celebrant and Subdeacon comes to meet them and, at the foot of the Altar, the Celebrant receives the Cross from the Deacon.

(When there are no Deacon and Subdeacon, the Celebrant goes to the sacristy with his servers, and from there he carries the Cross to the foot of the Altar, as above.)

The Holy Cross is uncovered as follows:

The Celebrant goes to the Epistle side of the sanctuary, stands facing the people and uncovers the Cross a little at the top. Then he intones the antiphon "Ecce lignum Crucis" alone; here he is joined by the Ministers, who sing with him up to "Veníte adorémus" which is sung by the Choir and all present.

When the singing is ended, all kneel, except the Celebrant, and adore silently for a brief moment.

The Celebrant next ascends to the Epistle side of the Altar and uncovers the right arm of the Cross; then, he elevates the Cross a little, aided by the Ministers if necessary, and sings "Ecce lignum Crucis" higher than before. The others join the singing at the same places noted above and kneel at its conclusion as before.

Finally, the Celebrant goes to the middle of the Altar, completely uncovers the Cross, elevates it, and sings "Ecce lignum Crucis" still higher. The others join in at the same places noted above and kneel in adoration after the singing.

Two Acolytes (or servers) with lighted candlesticks accompany the Cross at the right and left of the Celebrant.

Ecce lignum Crucis, in quo salus mundi pepéndit. | Behold the wood of the Cross, on which hung the Savior of the world.

All respond:

Veníte adorémus. | Come, let us adore.

After the Cross has been uncovered, the solemn Adoration of the Holy Cross begins as follows: The Celebrant gives the uncovered Cross to two Acolytes (or servers) who stand on the predella at the middle of the Altar and, facing the people, holds the Cross by the arms so that its foot rests on the predella. The two other Acolytes (or servers) with the lighted candles, remain kneeling on each side of the predella on the top step, facing the Cross.

Then the Cross is adored as follows: first comes the Celebrant alone, then the Ministers, next the Clergy, and finally the servers. All of these first remove their shoes (if it is convenient), and one by one approach the Cross, genuflect three times and kiss the feet of the Crucified.

When the Celebrant, Ministers, Clergy and servers have adored the Cross, it is taken to the Altar railing by the two Acolytes (or servers), accompanied by the other two Acolytes (or servers) carrying the lighted candlesticks. There, it is held in an upright position, so that the faithful, passing before the Cross in a kind of procession with men first and then women, may devoutly kiss the feet of the Crucified after making a simple genuflection.

While the Adoration of the Holy Cross takes place, the Choir divides into two parts and sings the so called Improperia or Reproaches and the other antiphons below. The Celebrant, Ministers and servers, and all who have completed the Adoration of the Holy Cross, sit and listen.

The singing of the "Reproaches" during the Adoration of the Holy Cross is prolonged for as long as the number of adorers requires. But it is always concluded with the doxology: "To God eternal glory be," etc., as on page 94.

Reproaches

The parts sung by the Choir are indicated by the numbers 1 (first Choir) and 2 (second Choir); those sung by both are indicated 1 and 2.

1 and 2 O My people, what have I done to thee, or wherein have I afflicted thee? Answer Me. ℣. Because I led thee out of the land of Egypt, thou hast prepared a Cross for thy Savior.

1 Agios, o Theos! *2* Sanctus Deus! (O Holy God!) *1* Agios ischyros! *2* Sanctus fortis! (O Holy strong One!) *1* Agios athanatos, eleison imas. *2* Sanctus immortalis, miserere nobis. (O Holy, immortal One, have mercy on us.)

1 and 2 Because I led thee out through the desert forty years, and fed thee with manna, and brought thee into a land exceeding good, thou hast prepared a Cross for thy Savior.

O Holy God! etc., *as above.*

1 and 2 What more ought I to have done for thee, than I have done? I planted thee, indeed, My most beautiful vineyard: and thou hast become exceeding bitter to Me: for in My thirst thou gavest Me vinegar to drink: and with a lance thou hast pierced the side of thy Savior.

O Holy God! etc., *as above.*

1 For thy sake I scourged Egypt with its firstborn: and thou hast scourged Me and delivered Me up.

2 O My people, what have I done to thee, or in what have I offended thee? Answer Me.

1 I led thee out of Egypt having drowned Pharao in the Red Sea: and thou hast delivered Me to the chief priests. *2* O My people, etc.

1 I opened the sea before thee: and thou with a spear hast opened My side. *2* O My people, etc.

1 I went before thee in a pillar of a cloud: and thou hast led Me to the judgment hall of Pilate. *2* O My people, etc.

1 I fed thee with manna in the desert: and thou hast beaten Me with blows and scourges. *2* O My people, etc.

1 I gave thee the water of salvation from the rock to drink: and thou hast given Me gall and vinegar. *2* O My people, etc.

1 For thy sake I struck the kings of the Chanaanites: and thou hast struck My head with a reed. *2* O My people, etc.

1 I gave thee a royal sceptre: and thou hast given to My head a crown of thorns. *2* O My people, etc.

1 I exalted thee with great strength: and thou hast hanged Me on the gibbet of the Cross. *2* O My people, etc.

1 and 2 Ant. We adore Thy Cross, O Lord, and we praise and glorify Thy holy Resurrection, for behold by that wood joy came into the whole world. *1 and 2 Ps. 66, 2.* May God have mercy on us, and bless us: may He cause the light of His countenance to shine upon us, and have mercy on us. *1 and 2* We adore, etc.

1 and 2 Ant. Faithful Cross, thou stand'st alone,
  None like thee in our woods is grown;
None can with thy rich growth compare,
  Or leaves like thine, or flowers bear.
Sweet wood, sweet nails, both sweet and fair,
  Sweet is the precious weight ye bear.

Hymn: Pange Lingua

1 Sing, O my tongue, the victor's praise,
  For Him the noblest trophy raise,
The victory of His Cross proclaim,
  His glory and His laurelled fame:
Sing of His conquests, when He proved
  The Savior of the souls He loved.

2 Faithful Cross, etc.

1 The great Creator, Lord of all,
  Pitying our parents' early fall,
When death from that destructive tree
  Rushed on them, and their progeny,
Would, by a tree, Himself make good
  The evils of that deadly wood.

2 Sweet wood, etc.

1 Order like this was just and meet,
  Poor man's redemption to complete,
That heavenly wisdom might destroy
  Our artful foe's malicious joy,
And from our evil's fatal spring
  A balsam for our wounds might bring.

2 Faithful Cross, etc.

1 Time's solemn plenitude was run
  When God sent forth His only Son
He Who the world's foundation laid,
  Born of a poor and lowly maid,
Came clothed in mortal flesh, and gave
  His life our fallen race to save.

2 Sweet wood, etc.

1 Beneath an infant-form debased,
  Within a lowly manger placed,
For us He weeps: and filled with grief

The Virgin's love would yield relief,
And fold Him with maternal care,
   To screen Him from the piercing air.

2 Faithful Cross, etc.

1 In pains and labors from His birth,
   Passed His appointed term on earth,
Freely our great Redeemer chose
   His sufferings and His mortal throes,
And as a lamb, whose blood is shed,
   A Victim on the Cross He bled.

2 Sweet wood, etc.

1 Gall is His drink, His spirit fails,
   Beneath the thorns and torturing nails;
The soldier's spear has brought a flood
   Of water mingled with His Blood:
A stream of grace and purest worth,
   To wash the deepened stains of earth.

2 Faithful Cross, etc.

1 O bend thy boughs, exalted tree,
   Relax thy stern rigidity:
An envied burden shalt thou bear,
   Receive it to thy tenderest care:
And gently take the precious load,
   The members of our King and God.

2 Sweet wood, etc.

1 Thou wert the worthy, chosen tree,
   The envied task was given to thee,
A Victim for the world to bear,
   An ark for sinners to prepare,
Stained with the Lamb's redeeming Blood,
   To save us from the whelming flood.

2 Faithful Cross, etc.

1 To God eternal glory be,
   In essence One, in Persons Three;
To each is highest honor meet,
   To Father, Son, and Paraclete:
May the whole world with joy proclaim
   Our God's adored and hallowed name. Amen.

2 Sweet wood, etc.

4th Part of the Liturgical Service—The Communion

After the Adoration of the Holy Cross, the Cross itself, which has been held by Acolytes (or servers), assisted by two other Acolytes (or servers) with lighted candlesticks, is carried back to the Altar, where it is placed in the middle, and if the structure of the Altar permits, as high as possible so that it can easily be seen by the people, unless the ceremonies about to take place on the Altar would render this inconvenient. Lighted candelabra are placed on the Altar.

Afterwards, when the Celebrant and Deacon have removed their black stoles, they put on purple vestments, namely, the Celebrant puts on the stole and chasuble; the Deacon puts on the stole and dalmatic, and the Subdeacon, the tunicle.

Then, after the Deacon places the burse on the Altar, he unfolds the corporal in the usual manner; moreover, an Acolyte (or server) places a cruet of water with a purificator on the Altar, for the purpose of washing and drying the fingers after Communion, and the book on the Gospel side.

(When there are no Deacon and Subdeacon, before the Procession begins, the Celebrant spreads the corporal on the Altar in the usual manner.)

After the above has been accomplished, the Blessed Sacrament is carried from the Repository to the Altar in order better to carry out the distribution of Holy Communion. Moreover, it is carried in the following manner:

The Celebrant, Subdeacon, Clergy, and people remain in their places in silence.

The Deacon with two Acolytes and another Cleric carrying the ombrellino goes to the Repository where there are two candlesticks with lighted candles, to be carried afterwards by the Acolytes.

They kneel at the Repository. Then the Deacon removes the pyx from the Tabernacle or Repository, and, having put on a white humeral veil, covers the pyx with the ends of the veil and proceeds to the main Altar.

(When there are no Deacon and Subdeacon, the Celebrant with his servers brings the Blessed Sacrament to the main Altar.)

They proceed in the same order as they came: the ombrellino is carried over the Blessed Sacrament; Acolytes hold lighted candlesticks; all fall to their knees. Meanwhile, the Choir sings the following antiphons:

1. We adore Thee, O Christ, and we bless Thee, because by Thy Cross Thou hast redeemed the world.

2. By the Wood we have become servants, and by the holy Cross we have been freed: the fruit of the tree has seduced us, and the Son of God has redeemed us.

3. O Savior of the world, save us: we pray Thee, our God, to help us, Who by Thy Cross and Blood hast redeemed us.

When they reach the main Altar, they ascend; the Deacon places the sacred pyx on the corporal and the Acolytes place the candlesticks on the Altar. Having genuflected, the Deacon removes the humeral veil and goes to the Epistle side; the Acolytes descend and genuflect on the bottom step of the Altar.

After adoring on both knees, the Celebrant and Subdeacon ascend the Altar, and after both genuflect, the Celebrant recites the preface to the Our Father.

The entire Our Father, since it is the prayer for Communion, is recited slowly and distinctly in Latin by all, laity and Clergy, together with the Celebrant.

The Celebrant alone, with joined hands, says:

Orémus. Præcéptis salutáribus móniti, et divína institutióne formáti, audémus dícere:

Let us pray. Prompted by saving precepts, and taught by Thy divine teaching, we dare to say:

The Celebrant with joined hands, and all present say:

Pater noster, qui es in cœlis: *

Sanctificétur nomen tuum. *

Advéniat regnum tuum. *

Fiat volúntas tua, sicut in cœlo, et in terra.*

Panem nostrum quotidiánum da nobis hódie: *

Our Father, Who art in heaven: *

Hallowed be Thy name. *

Thy kingdom come. *

Thy will be done on earth as it is in heaven.*

Give us this day our daily bread: *

Et dimítte nobis débita nostra, *	And forgive us our trespasses, *
Sicut et nos dimíttimus debitóribus, nostris. *	As we forgive those who trespass against us.*
Et ne nos indúcas in tentatiónem; *	And lead us not into temptation; *
Sed líbera nos a malo. *	But deliver us from evil. *
Amen.	Amen.

Deliver us, we beseech Thee, O Lord, from all evils, past, present, and to come; and by the intercession of the Blessed and Glorious Mary, ever Virgin, Mother of God, together with Thy Blessed Apostles, Peter and Paul, and Andrew, and all the Saints, grant of Thy goodness, peace in our days: that, aided by the riches of Thy mercy, we may be always free from sin, and safe from all disturbance. Through the same Jesus Christ, Thy Son, our Lord. Who with Thee liveth and reigneth in the unity of the Holy Ghost, God, world without end. *All respond*: Amen.

The Celebrant continues in a low voice:

Let not the partaking of Thy Body, O Lord Jesus Christ, which I, though unworthy, presume to receive, turn to my judgment and condemnation; but through Thy goodness, may it become a safeguard and an effective remedy, both of soul and body. Who livest and reignest with God the Father, in the unity of the Holy Ghost, God, world without end. Amen.

Lord, I am not worthy that Thou shouldst come under my roof; but only say the word, and my soul will be healed. (3 *times*.)

Signing himself with the Blessed Sacrament, he says:

May the Body of our Lord Jesus Christ keep my soul unto life everlasting. Amen.

He reverently consumes the Sacred Host and remains a short time in meditation.

The Deacon recites the "Confiteor" as usual. Then the Celebrant pronounces the absolution, to which all respond: "Amen." Then holding up a Sacred Host and turning toward the people, he says: "Behold the Lamb," etc., and "Lord, I am not worthy," etc., as usual.

Holy Communion is distributed in the same manner as on Holy Thursday. The Priests remove their purple stoles.

After Holy Communion is distributed, the Celebrant purifies his fingers in a bowl and wipes them with the purificator in silence; he replaces the ciborium in the Tabernacle.

The Celebrant says the following three prayers in a ferial tone with hands joined. All stand and respond "Amen" after each prayer.

Let us pray. May Thy blessing, we beseech Thee, O Lord, descend copiously upon Thy people, who have devoutly recalled the Passion and Death of Thy Son, may Thy kindness come upon them, may Thy consolation be bestowed on them, may their holy faith increasingly grow, may their eternal redemption be strengthened. Through the same Christ our Lord. ℟. Amen.

Let us pray. Almighty and merciful God, Who, by the blessed Passion and Death of Christ hast redeemed us: preserve in us the work of Thy mercy; that, through participation in this mystery, we may live in everlasting devotion. Through the same Christ our Lord. ℟. Amen.

Let us pray. O Lord, remember Thy mercies, and sanctify Thy children with everlasting protection, for whom Christ, Thy Son, by His own Blood, instituted the paschal mystery. Through the same Christ our Lord. ℟. Amen.

The Celebrant and sacred Ministers descend the Altar, genuflect together with the Acolytes (or servers), and return to the sacristy.

At a convenient time, the Most Holy Eucharist is carried privately to the place where it is reserved, and the sanctuary lamp is lighted. The Altar is stripped.

"He is not here, for He has risen   "

HOLY SATURDAY — THE EASTER VIGIL

Priv. Feria, Dbl. 1st Cl.   Purple and White

Station: St. John Lateran

This is the day of the most intense sorrow, the day on which the Church tarries at the Lord's tomb, meditating about His Passion and Death.

While the Altar remains stripped, the Church abstains from the Sacrifice of the Mass until. after the solemn vigil or the nocturnal wait for the Resurrection, there come the Easter joys, the abundance of which carries over to the days that follow.

The intention and the purpose of this vigil is to point out and to recall how our life and grace have flowed from the Lord's Death. And so, our Lord Himself is shown under the sign of the paschal candle as "the light of the World" *(John 13, 12),* Who has put the darkness of our sins to flight by the grace of His light.

The "Paschal Proclamation" is sung in which the splendor of the holy night of the Resurrection is glorified.

The wonderful works done by God under the old alliance. pale imaginings of the marvels done under the new covenant, are recalled.

There is the blessing of the baptismal water, in which "buried together with Christ" unto the death of sin, we rise again with the same Christ so that "we may walk in newness of life" *(Rom. 6, 4).*

Then we promise, by the renewal of our baptismal vows, to bear witness before all, by our lives and our conduct, to this grace which Christ has merited for us and which He confers upon us in Baptism.

Finally, after we implore the intercession of the Church triumphant, the sacred vigil ends with the solemn Mass of the Resurrection. *(Decree of S.C.R., Nov. 16, 1955.)*

The Blessing of the New Fire

At a convenient hour, so as to allow the Solemn Mass of the Easter Vigil to start around midnight, the Altars are covered with altar cloths, but the candles are not lighted until the beginning of the Mass. Meanwhile fire is struck from a flint and charcoal is kindled from it.

The Celebrant is vested with amice, alb, cincture, purple stole and cope; the sacred Ministers, with amice, alb and cincture: the Deacon with stole and dalmatic, and the Subdeacon with tunicle of the same color.

(When there are no Deacon and Subdeacon, the Celebrant is vested with amice, alb, cincture, purple stole and cope, or without the chasuble.)

While the Ministers (or servers) stand nearby with Cross, holy water and incense, either outside the entrance of the church, or in the vestibule, or inside the church, wherever the people can better follow the sacred rite, the Celebrant blesses the new fire, saying:

℣. The Lord be with you. ℟. And with thy spirit.

Let us pray. O God, Who hast bestowed on the faithful the fire of Thy brightness through Thy Son, Who is the cornerstone, sanctify ✠ this new fire produced from a flint that it may be profitable to us, and grant that during this Paschal festival we may be so inflamed with heavenly desires, that with pure minds we may come to the solemnity of perpetual light. Through the same Christ our Lord. ℟. Amen.

Then he sprinkles the fire with holy water three times, without saying anything.

The Acolyte (or one of the servers), taking some of the blessed charcoal, puts it into the thurible; then the Celebrant places incense in the thurible, blessing it in the usual manner, and incenses the fire three times.

The Blessing of the Paschal Candle

After the blessing of the new fire, the Acolyte (or one of the servers) brings the Paschal Candle to the middle, in front of the Celebrant, who incises a Cross in the wax with a stylus (or knife), between the points where the grains of incense will be inserted. Then he carves the Greek letter Alpha above the Cross and the Greek letter Omega below the Cross, and, between the arms of the Cross, the four numerals of the current year. While carving these symbols he says respectively:

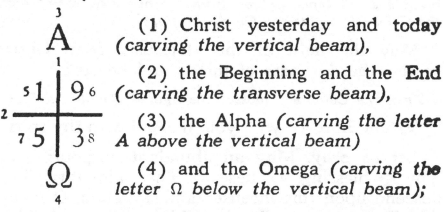

(1) Christ yesterday and today (carving the vertical beam),

(2) the Beginning and the End (carving the transverse beam),

(3) the Alpha (carving the letter A above the vertical beam)

(4) and the Omega (carving the letter Ω below the vertical beam);

(5) to Him belongs Time (as he carves the first numeral of the current year in the upper left-hand angle of the Cross)

(6) and the ages (as he carves the second numeral of the current year in the upper right-hand angle of the Cross);

(7) to Him be glory and empire (as he carves the third numeral of the current year in the lower left-hand angle of the Cross, for example, 5)

(8) throughout all the ages of eternity. Amen (as he carves the fourth numeral of the current year in the lower right-hand angle of the Cross, for example, 3).

After the Cross and other symbols have been carved, the Deacon (or one of the servers) gives the grains of incense to the Celebrant. If they are not already blessed, the Celebrant sprinkles them three times with holy water and incenses them three times, in silence. Then he inserts the five grains into the places prepared for them, meanwhile saying:

```
    1
 4  2  5
    3
```

(1) Through His holy wounds

(2) glorious

(3) may He guard

(4) and protect us

(5) Christ the Lord. Amen.

Then the Deacon (or one of the servers) gives the Celebrant a small taper lighted from the new fire, with which the Celebrant lights the Candle, saying:

May the light of the gloriously risen Christ scatter the darkness of minds and hearts.

Then the Celebrant blesses the lighted Candle, saying:

℣. The Lord be with you. ℟. And with thy spirit.

Let us pray. May an abundant outpouring of Thy ✠ blessing, we beseech Thee, almighty God, descend upon this incense: and do Thou, O invisible Regenerator, illumine this nocturnal brightness, that not only the sacrifice that is offered this night may shine by the secret mixture of Thy light, but also into whatever place anything of this mysterious sanctification shall be brought, there, the power of Thy Majesty may be present and all the malicious artifices of Satan may be defeated. Through Christ our Lord. ℟. Amen.

Meanwhile, all the lights of the church are put out.

The Procession and Paschal Proclamation

The Deacon, vested in white stole and dalmatic, takes the lighted Paschal Candle and the Procession is formed: the Thurifer leads, followed by the Subdeacon with Cross, the Deacon with the lighted Paschal Candle, immediately after him the Celebrant, and then the Clergy and people.

(When there are no Deacon and Subdeacon, the Celebrant lays aside his purple vestments, vests in white stole and dalmatic, takes the lighted Paschal Candle and the Procession is formed: the Thurifer leads, followed by the Crossbearer, immediately followed by the Celebrant carrying the Paschal Candle, then servers and people.)

When the Deacon has entered the church, he raises the Paschal Candle, and, standing erect, he intones:

Lumen Christi (The Light of Christ),

to which everyone in the church, except the Subdeacon and Thurifer, genuflecting toward the Paschal Candle, responds:

Deo Grátias (Thanks be to God).

Here, the Celebrant lights his own candle from the Paschal Candle. (When there are no Deacon and Subdeacon, one of the servers lights a taper from the Paschal Candle and carries it for the Celebrant.)

Proceeding to the middle of the church, the Deacon, standing erect, again intones in a higher key: "Lumen Christi," to which everyone in the church, genuflecting toward the Paschal Candle, responds: "Deo Gratias." Here, the candles of the Clergy (or of the servers) are lighted from the Paschal Candle.

Thirdly, the Deacon proceeds to the Altar, and in the middle of the sanctuary, he intones in a still higher key: "Lumen Christi," to which, for the third time, everyone in the church, genuflecting toward the Paschal Candle, responds: "Deo Gratias." Here, all the candles of the people are lighted from the Paschal Candle and the lights of the church are put on.

The Celebrant then goes to his place in the sanctuary on the Epistle side; the Subdeacon with Cross stands at the Gospel side; and the Clergy take their places on the benches.

The Deacon fixes the Paschal Candle on a small stand in the middle of the sanctuary, and, taking the Missal, he asks a blessing from the Celebrant, as it is done at the Gospel during Mass. The Celebrant says:

The Lord be in your heart and on your lips, that you may worthily and fittingly proclaim His paschal praise: In the name of the Father, and of the Son, ✠ and of the Holy Ghost. Amen.

(When there are no Deacon and Subdeacon, the Celebrant fixes the Paschal Candle on a small stand in the middle of the sanctuary, and goes to the credence table; the Cross-

bearer goes to the Gospel side; the remaining servers take their places within the sanctuary. The Celebrant takes the Missal from the credence table. and kneeling on the steps of the Altar says only: "Pray, Lord, Thy blessing. The Lord be in my heart and on my lips, that I may worthily and fittingly proclaim His paschal praise. Amen.")

The Deacon now goes to the lectern, which is covered with a white cloth. He places the Missal on it, and incenses it; then, he incenses the Paschal Candle, going around it as he does so.

Now, while all rise and stand, as at the Gospel, the Deacon sings the Paschal Proclamation—facing the Paschal Candle, the Altar at his right and the congregation at his left. (When there are no Deacon and Subdeacon, the Celebrant does the same.)

The Paschal Proclamation

Let the angelic choirs of heaven now rejoice; let the divine mysteries give praise; and let the trumpet of salvation sound forth the victory of so great a King. Let the earth also rejoice, made radiant by such splendor; and, enlightened with the brightness of the eternal King, let it know that the darkness of the whole world is scattered. Let our Mother the Church also rejoice, adorned with the brightness of so great a light; and let this temple resound with the loud acclamations of the people. Wherefore I beseech you, most beloved brethren, who are here present in the wondrous brightness of this holy light, to invoke with me the mercy of almighty God, that He Who has deigned to admit me among the Levites, without any merits of mine, would pour forth the brightness of His light upon me, and enable me to perfect the praise of this wax candle. Through our Lord Jesus Christ His Son, Who liveth and reigneth with Him and the Holy Spirit, one God.

℣. World without end. ℟. Amen.

℣. The Lord be with you. ℟. And with thy spirit.

℣. Lift up your hearts. ℟. We have them lifted up unto the Lord.

℣. Let us give thanks unto the Lord our God. ℟. It is fitting and just.

It is fitting indeed and just to proclaim with all our hearts and all the affection of our minds, and with the ministry of our voices, the invisible **God, the Father Almighty,** and His Only-begotten Son our Lord, Jesus Christ, Who repaid for us to His Eternal Father the debt of Adam, and by the merciful shedding of His Blood, cancelled the guilt incurred by original sin. For this is the Paschal Festival, in which that true Lamb is slain, with Whose Blood the doorposts of the faithful are consecrated. This is the night in which Thou didst formerly cause our forefathers, the children of Israel, when brought out of Egypt, to pass through the Red Sea, with dry feet. This, therefore, is the night which dissipated the darkness of sinners by the light of the pillar. This is the night which at this time, throughout the world, restores to grace and unites in sanctity those who believe in Christ, and are separated from the vices of the world and the darkness of sinners. This is the night in which, destroying the chains of death, Christ arose victorious from the grave. For it would have profited us nothing to have been born, unless redemption had also been bestowed upon us. O wondrous condescension of Thy mercy toward us! O inestimable affection of love, that Thou mightest redeem a slave, Thou didst deliver up Thy Son! O truly needful sin of Adam, which was blotted out by the death of Christ! O happy fault, that merited to have such and so great a Redeemer! O truly blessed night, which alone deserved to know the time and hour when Christ rose again from the dead! This is the night of which it is written: And the night shall be as clear as the day; and the night is my light in my pleasures. Therefore the sanctification of this night puts to flight all wickedness, cleanses sins, and restores innocence to the fallen, and gladness to the sorrowful. It drives forth hatreds, it prepares concord, and brings down haughtiness.

Therefore, in this sacred night, receive, O holy Father, the evening sacrifice of this incense, which Holy Church renders to Thee by the hands of Thy Ministers in the solemn offering of this wax candle, the work of bees. Now also we know the praises of this column, which the glowing fire enkindles to the honor of God. Which fire, although divided into parts, suffers no loss from its light being borrowed. For it is nourished by the melting wax, which the mother bee produced for the substance of this precious light. O truly blessed night, which plundered the Egyptians and enriched the Hebrews! A night in which heavenly things are united to those of earth, and things divine to those which are human.

We beseech Thee, therefore, O Lord, that this wax candle, sanctified in honor of Thy name, may continue to burn to dissipate the darkness of this night. And being accepted as an odor of sweetness, may it be united with the heavenly lights. Let the morning star find its flame alight; that star, I mean, which knows no setting, He Who returning from the grave, serenely shone forth upon mankind. We beseech Thee therefore, O Lord, that Thou wouldst grant a peaceful season during these Paschal solemnities, and deign to rule, govern, and protect with Thy constant protection Thy servants, and all the Clergy, and the devout people, together with our most Holy Father, Pope N., and our Bishop N. Look down also upon those who rule over us, and, with Thy unspeakable gift of kindness and mercy, direct their thoughts to justice and peace, that, after their earthly toil, they may attain their heavenly abode together with all Thy people. Through the same Jesus Christ, Thy Son, our Lord, Who liveth and reigneth with Thee, in the unity of the Holy Spirit, one God, world without end. ℟. Amen.

The Lessons

After the Paschal Proclamation, the Deacon lays aside his white vestments, puts on purple vestments, and goes to the Celebrant. (When there are no Deacon and Subdeacon, the Celebrant lays aside his white dalmatic and stole, puts on purple cope and stole, and goes to the lectern.)

Then the Lessons are read, omitting the title and "Thanks be to God" at the end of each Lesson. They are read by a Lector, who stands in the middle of the sanctuary, in front of the Paschal Candle, with the Altar on his right and the congregation at his left. The Celebrant, Ministers, Clergy and people sit and listen. (When there are no Deacon and Subdeacon, the Celebrant himself reads the Lessons. If there is a Lector who is a Cleric, then all is accomplished as above.)

At the end of each Lesson, or after the Canticle, the prayers are said in the following manner: all rise; the Celebrant says, "Let us pray"; the Deacon subjoins, "Let us kneel," and all kneel in silent prayer for some time. When the Deacon says, "Arise," all rise and the Celebrant says the prayer. (If the Celebrant himself reads the Lessons, he himself says, "Let us pray," "Let us kneel," and "Arise.")

First Lesson. *Gen. 1, 1-31; 2, 1-2.* In the beginning God created heaven and earth. And the earth was void and empty, and darkness was upon the face of the deep: and the Spirit of God moved over the waters. And God said: Be light made. And light was made. And God saw the light that it was good: and He divided the light from the darkness. And He called the light Day, and the darkness Night: and there was evening and morning, one day. And God said: Let there be a firmament made amidst the waters: and let it divide the waters from the waters. And God made a firmament, and divided the waters that were under the firmament from those that were above the firmament. And it was so. And God called the firmament Heaven: and the evening and morning were the second day. God also said: Let the waters that are under the heavens be gathered together into one place; and let the dry land appear. And it was so done. And God called the dry land Earth: and the gathering together of the waters He called Seas. And God saw that it was good. And He said: Let the earth bring forth the green herb, and such as may seed, and the fruit tree yielding fruit after its kind, which may have seed in itself upon the earth. And it was so done. And the earth brought forth the green herb, and such as yields seed according to its kind, and the tree that bears fruit, having seed, each one according to its kind. And God saw that it was good. And the evening and the morning were the third day. And God said: Let there be lights made in the firmament of heaven to divide the day and the night, and let them be for signs, and for seasons, and for days and years: to shine in the firmament of heaven, and to give light upon the earth. And it was so done. And God made two great lights: a greater light to rule the day, and a lesser light to rule the night: and the stars. And He set them in the firmament of heaven, to shine upon the earth, and to rule the day and the night, and to divide the light and the darkness. And God saw that it was good. And the evening and morning were the fourth day. God also said: Let the waters bring forth the creeping creatures having life, and the fowl that may fly over the earth under the firmament of heaven. And God created the great whales, and every living and moving creature which the waters brought forth, according to their kinds, and every winged fowl according to its kind. And God saw that it was good. And He blessed them, saying: Increase and multiply, and fill the waters of the sea: and let the birds be multiplied upon the earth. And the evening and the morning were the fifth day. And God said: Let the earth bring forth the living creatures in its kind, cattle, and creeping things, and beasts of the earth according to their kinds. And it was so done. And God made the beasts of the earth according to their kinds, and cattle, and everything that creeps on the earth after its kind. And God saw that it was good. And He said: Let us make man to Our image and likeness: and let him have dominion over the fishes of the sea, and the fowls of the air, and the beasts, and the whole earth, and every creeping creature that moves upon the earth. And God created man to His own image: to the image of God He created him, male and female He created them. And God blessed them, saying: Increase and multiply, and fill the earth, and subdue it, and rule over the fishes of the sea, and the fowls of the air, and all living creatures that move upon the earth. And God said: Behold, I have given you every herb bearing seed upon the earth, and all trees that have in themselves seed of their own kind, to be your meat: and to all beasts of the earth, and to every fowl of the air, and to all that move upon the earth, and wherein there is life, that they may have to feed upon. And it was so done. And God saw all the things that He had made, and they were very good. And the evening and morning were the sixth day. So the heavens and the earth were finished, and all the furniture of them. And on the seventh day God ended His work which He had made: and He rested on the seventh day from all His work which He had done.

Let us pray. ℣. Let us kneel. ℞. Arise. O God, Who hast wonderfully created man, and more wonderfully redeemed him; grant us, we beseech Thee, to stand firm with strong minds against the allurements of sin, that we may be worthy to arrive at everlasting joys. Through our Lord Jesus Christ, Thy Son, Who liveth and reigneth with Thee in the unity of the Holy Spirit, God, world without end. ℞. Amen. ⤵

Second Lesson. *Ex. 14, 24-31; 15, 1.* In those days, the morning watch was come, and behold the Lord looking upon the Egyptian army through the pillar of fire, and of the cloud, slew their host, and overthrew the wheels of the chariots, and they were carried into the deep. And the Egyptians said: Let us flee from Israel: for the Lord fights for them against us. And the Lord said to Moses: Stretch forth thy hand over the sea, that the waters may come again upon the Egyptians, upon their chariots and horsemen. And when Moses had stretched forth his hand toward the sea, it returned at the first break of day to the former place: and as the Egyptians were fleeing away, the waters came upon them, and the Lord shut them up in the middle of the waves. And the waters returned, and covered the chariots and the horsemen of all the army of Pharao, who had come into the sea after them, neither did there so much as one of them remain. But the children of Israel marched through the midst of the sea upon dry land, and the waters were to them as a wall on the right hand and on the left: and the Lord delivered Israel on that day out of the hand of the Egyptians. And they saw the Egyptians dead upon the seashore, and the mighty hand that the Lord had used against them: and the people feared the Lord, and they believed the Lord, and Moses His servant. Then Moses and the children of Israel sung this canticle to the Lord, and said:

Canticle. *Ex. 15, 1. 2.* Let us sing to the Lord, for He is gloriously magnified: the horse and the rider He has thrown into the sea: He is become my Helper and Protector unto salvation. ℣. He is my God, and I will glorify Him: the God of my father, and I will exalt Him. ℣. The Lord crushes wars: the Lord is His name.

Let us pray. ℣. Let us kneel. ℟. Arise. O God, Whose ancient miracles we see shining even in our times: since what by the power of Thy right hand Thou didst confer upon one people by delivering them from Egyptian persecution, Thou dost operate by the water of regeneration for the salvation of the Gentiles; grant that the fullness of the whole world may pass over to the children of Abraham, and the dignity of Israelites. Through our Lord Jesus Christ, Thy Son, Who liveth and reigneth with Thee in the unity of the Holy Spirit, God, world without end. ℟. Amen. ➤

Third Lesson. *Isa. 4, 2-6.* In that day the bud of the Lord shall be in magnificence and glory, and the fruit of the earth shall be high, and a great joy to them that shall have escaped of Israel. And it shall come to pass, that everyone who shall be left in Sion, and who shall remain in Jerusalem, shall be called holy, everyone who is written in life in Jerusalem, if the Lord shall wash away the filth of the daughters of Sion, and shall wash away the blood of Jerusalem out of the midst thereof, by the spirit of judgment and by the spirit of burning. And the Lord will create upon every place of Mount Sion, and where He is called upon, a cloud by day, and a smoke and the brightness of a flaming fire in the night: for over all the glory shall be a protection. And there shall be a tabernacle for a shade in the daytime from the heat, and for a security and covert from the whirlwind and from rain. ⇁

Canticle. *Isa. 5, 1. 2. 7.* The beloved had a vineyard on a hill in a fruitful place. ℣. And he enclosed it with a wall, and dug round about it, and planted the vine of Sorec, and built a tower in the midst thereof. ℣. And he dug a winepress therein: for the vineyard of the Lord of Hosts is the house of Israel.

Let us pray. ℣. Let us kneel. ℟. Arise. O God, Who by the voice of the holy Prophets hast declared to all the children of Thy Church that through the whole extent of Thy dominion, Thou art the Sower of good seed and the Cultivator of chosen branches; grant to Thy people who are called by Thee by the names of vines and cornfields, that they may root out all thorns and briars, and produce good fruit in abundance. Through our Lord Jesus Christ, Thy Son, Who liveth and reigneth with Thee in the unity of the Holy Spirit, God, world without end. ℟. Amen. ⇁

Fourth Lesson. *Deut. 31, 22-30.* In those days, Moses wrote a canticle, and taught it to the children of Israel. And the Lord commanded Josue the son of Nun, and said: Take courage, and be valiant: for thou shalt bring the children of Israel into the land which I have promised, and I will be with thee. Therefore, after Moses wrote the words of this law in a volume, and finished it: he commanded the Levites, who carried the ark of the covenant of the Lord, saying: Take this book and put it in the side of the ark of the covenant of the Lord your God: that it may be there for a testimony against thee. For I know thy obstinacy and thy most stiff neck. While I am yet living, and going in with you, you have always been rebellious against the Lord: how much more when I shall be dead? Gather unto me all the ancients of your tribes and your doctors, and I will speak these words in their hearing, and will call heaven and earth to witness against them. For I know that after my death you will do wickedly and will quickly turn aside from the way that I have commanded you: and evils shall come upon you in the latter times, when you shall do evil in the sight of the Lord, to provoke Him by the works of your hands. Moses therefore spoke in the hearing of the whole assembly of Israel the words of this canticle, and finished it even to the end. ⤵

Canticle. *Deut. 32, 1-4.* Hear, O heaven, and I will speak: and let the earth give ear to the words out of my mouth. ℣. Let my speech be expected like rain: and my words descend like dew. ℣. As a shower upon the grass, and like snow upon hay: because I will invoke the name of the Lord. ℣. Give ye magnificence to our God: God's works are true, and all His ways are judgments. ℣. God is faithful, in Whom there is no iniquity: the Lord is just and holy.

Let us pray. ℣. Let us kneel. ℟. Arise. O God, the exaltation of the humble, and the strength of the righteous, Who, by Thy holy servant Moses, wast pleased so to instruct Thy people by the singing of Thy sacred canticle, that that renewal of the law should be also our guidance, stir up Thy power in all the fullness of the justified Gentiles, and give joy whilst Thou dost diminish fear; that, all sins being blotted out by Thy remission, what was denounced in vengeance, may be conducive to our salvation. Through our Lord Jesus Christ, Thy

Son, Who liveth and reigneth with Thee in the unity of the Holy Spirit, God, world without end. ℟. Amen.

The First Part of the Litany of the Saints

When the Lessons are finished, two Cantors sing the Litany of the Saints up to the invocation "Propítius esto" (Be merciful to us). The people kneel and sing the responses. (If there are no Cantors, the Priest himself sings the Litany while kneeling on the lowest Altar step and the people kneel and sing the responses.)

Kýrie eléison.
Lord, have mercy.

Christe eléison.
Christ, have mercy.

Kýrie eléison.
Lord, have mercy.

Christe, audi nos.
Christ, hear us.

Christe, exáudi nos.
Christ, graciously hear us.

Pater de cælis, Deus, *miserére nobis.*
God the Father of heaven, *have mercy on us.*

Fili, Redémptor mundi, Deus, *miserére nobis.*
God the Son, Redeemer of the world, *have mercy on us.*

Spíritus Sancte, Deus, *miserére nobis.*
God the Holy Spirit, *have mercy on us.*

Sancta Trínitas, unus Deus, *miserére nobis.*
Holy Trinity, one God, *have mercy on us.*

Sancta María,*
Holy Mary,*

Sancta Dei Génitrix,
Holy Mother of God,

Sancta Virgo vírginum,
Holy Virgin of virgins,

Sancte Míchaël,
St. Michael,

Sancte Gábriel,
St. Gabriel,

Sancte Ráphaël,
St. Raphael,

Omnes sancti Angeli et Archángeli,**
All ye holy Angels and Archangels,

Omnes sancti beatórum Spirítuum órdines,
All ye holy orders of blessed Spirits,

Sancte Joánnes Baptísta,*
St. John the Baptist,

Sancte Joseph,
St. Joseph,

*Ora pro nobis.
**Oráte pro nobis.

*Pray for us.

Omnes sancti Patriárchæ et Prophétæ,** — All ye holy Patriarchs and Prophets,*

Sancte Petre,* — St. Peter,

Sancte Paule, — St. Paul,

Sancte Andréa, — St. Andrew,

Sancte Joánnes, — St. John,

Omnes sancti Apóstoli et Evangelístæ,** — All ye holy Apostles and Evangelists,

Omnes sancti Discípuli Dómini, — All ye holy Disciples of our Lord,

Sancte Stéphane,* — St. Stephen,

Sancte Laurénti, — St. Lawrence,

Sancte Vincénti, — St. Vincent,

Omnes sancti Mártyres,** — All ye holy Martyrs,

Sancte Silvéster,* — St. Sylvester,

Sancte Gregóri, — St. Gregory,

Sancte Augustíne, — St. Augustine,

Omnes sancti Pontífices et Confessóres,** — All ye holy Bishops and Confessors,

Omnes sancti Doctóres, — All ye holy Doctors,

Sancte Antóni,* — St. Anthony,

Sancte Benedícte, — St. Benedict,

Sancte Domínice, — St. Dominic,

Sancte Francísce, — St. Francis,

Omnes sancti Sacerdótes et Levítæ,** — All ye holy Priests and Levites,

Omnes sancti Mónachi et Eremítæ, — All ye holy Monks and Hermits,

Sancta María Magdaléna,* — St. Mary Magdalene,

Sancta Agnes, — St. Agnes,

Sancta Cæcília, — St. Cecilia,

Sancta Agatha, — St. Agatha,

Sancta Anastásia, — St. Anastasia,

Omnes sanctæ Virgines et Víduæ,** — All ye holy Virgins and Widows,

Omnes Sancti et Sanctæ Dei, *intercédite pro nobis.* — All ye holy men and women, Saints of God, *make intercession for us.*

---

*Ora pro nobis.

**Oráte pro nobis.

---

*Pray for us.

If the church has no Baptismal Font, the ceremony continues on page 121, with the Renewal of Baptismal Promises, otherwise as below.

The Blessing of the Baptismal Water within the Sanctuary

NOTE: For the Blessing of the Baptismal Water when Baptistery is apart from the church, the blessing is the same, except that while the Celebrant proceeds to the Baptistery, the Canticle, page 120, is sung, and before he enters the Baptistery he says the prayer, page 121.

While the Litany of the Saints is being sung, the vessel containing the Baptismal Water and everything necessary for its blessing, are prepared in the middle of the sanctuary, on the Epistle side, in view of all the people.

The Celebrant stands facing the people with the vessel of Baptismal Water before him; at his right, the Paschal Candle; and at his left, another Subdeacon or Cleric (or server), with Cross. In a ferial tone, the Celebrant says:

℣. The Lord be with you. ℟. And with thy spirit.

Let us pray. Almighty and everlasting God, be present at these mysteries of Thy great goodness, be present at these sacraments: and send forth the spirit of adoption to regenerate the new people, whom the font of baptism brings forth to Thee; that what is to be done by our humble ministry may be accomplished by the effect of Thy power. Through our Lord Jesus Christ, Thy Son, Who liveth and reigneth with Thee in the unity of the Holy Spirit, God:

The Celebrant raises his voice to the tone of the Preface, and joining his hands, he continues:

℣. World without end. ℟. Amen.

℣. The Lord be with you. ℟. And with thy spirit.

℣. Lift up your hearts. ℟. We have lifted them up to the Lord.

℣. Let us give thanks to the Lord our God. ℟. It is fitting and just.

It is fitting indeed and just, right and helpful to salvation, for us always and everywhere to give

Thee thanks, O Holy Lord, Father Almighty, Everlasting God, Who by Thy invisible power dost wonderfully produce the effect of Thy sacraments. And though we are unworthy to perform such great mysteries, yet, as Thou dost not abandon the gifts of Thy grace, so Thou inclinest the ears of Thy goodness, even to our prayers. O God, Whose Spirit in the very beginning of the world moved over the waters, that even then the nature of water might receive the virtue of sanctification; O God, Who by water didst wash away the crimes of the guilty world, and by the pouring out of the deluge didst give a figure of regeneration, that one and the same element might in a mystery be the end of vice and the beginning of virtue; look, O Lord, on the face of Thy Church, and multiply in her Thy regenerations, Who by the streams of Thy abundant grace fillest Thy city with joy, and dost open the font of Baptism for the renewal of the Gentiles throughout the world: that by the command of Thy Majesty she may receive the grace of Thy Only-begotten Son from the Holy Spirit.

Here the Celebrant with outstretched hand, divides the water in the form of a Cross, dries his hand immediately with a towel, and says:

May He, by a secret mixture of His divine power, render this water fruitful for the regeneration of men, so that a heavenly offspring, conceived in sanctification, may emerge from the immaculate womb of this divine font, reborn a new creature; and grace as a mother may bring forth everyone, however distinguished either by sex in body, or by age in time, to the same infancy. Therefore, may all unclean spirits, by Thy command, O Lord, depart far from hence; may the whole malice of diabolical deceit be entirely banished; may no admixture of the enemy's power prevail here; let him not fly about to lay his snares; may he not creep in unperceived; may he not corrupt with infection.

He touches the water with his hand.

May this holy and innocent creature be free from all the assaults of the enemy, and purified by the destruction of all his wickedness. May it be a living fountain, a regenerating water, a purifying stream, that all those who are to be washed in this saving bath may obtain, by the operation of the Holy Spirit, the grace of a perfect cleansing.

Here the Celebrant makes the Sign of the Cross three times over the water, saying:

Wherefore I bless thee, O creature of water, by the living ✠ God, by the true ✠ God, by the holy ✠ God, by that God Who in the beginning, by His word, separated thee from the dry land, Whose Spirit moved over thee.

Here he divides the water with his hand, and throws some of it toward the north, south, east and west, saying:

Who made thee flow from the fountain of paradise and commanded thee to water the whole earth in four rivers. Who, changing thy bitterness in the desert into sweetness, made thee fit to drink, and produced thee from a rock to quench the thirsty people. I bless ✠ thee also by Jesus Christ His only Son, our Lord, Who, in Cana of Galilee changed thee into wine by a wonderful miracle. Who walked with His feet upon thee, and was baptized in thee by John in the Jordan. Who made thee flow out of His side together with His Blood, and commanded His disciples, that such as believed should be baptized in thee, saying: Go, teach all nations, baptizing them in the name of the Father, and of the Son, and of the Holy Ghost.

He lowers his voice and continues in a speaking tone:

Do Thou, almighty and merciful God, be present with us who observe these precepts: do Thou graciously inspire us.

He breathes three times upon the water in the form of a Cross, saying:

Do Thou with Thy mouth bless these clear waters, that besides their natural power of cleansing bodies, they may also prove efficacious for the purification of souls.

Here the Celebrant dips the Paschal Candle a little in the water, and singing in the tone of the Preface says:

May the power of the Holy Spirit descend into all the water of this font.

He then withdraws the Paschal Candle from the water, and immerses it again to a greater depth, repeating in a higher tone "May the power," etc.

Again he withdraws the Paschal Candle from the water, and for the third time immerses it down to the bottom, repeating in a higher tone still, "May the power," etc. Then breathing three times over the water in the form of the Greek letter Ψ he continues:

And may He render the whole substance of this water fruitful with the quality of regeneration.

Here the Paschal Candle is taken out of the water, and the Celebrant continues:

Here may the stains of all sins be washed away; here may human nature, created in Thy image, and reformed to the honor of its origin, be cleansed from all the filth of its old state, that all who receive this sacrament of regeneration, may be born again to a new infancy of true innocence.

The following is said in a reading tone:

Through our Lord Jesus Christ Thy Son: Who will come to judge the living and the dead, and the world by fire. ℟. Amen.

Then one of the Clerics (or servers) takes some of the same water in a container, to be used to sprinkle the people after the Renewal of Baptismal Promises, page 121, and for sprinkling homes and other places.

When this has been done, the Celebrant pours some of the Oil of Catechumens into the water in the form of a Cross, saying audibly:

May this font be sanctified and made fruitful by the oil of salvation, for those who are born anew therein unto life everlasting. R̂. Amen.

Then the Celebrant pours in Chrism in the same way.

May the infusion of the Chrism of our Lord Jesus Christ, and of the Holy Ghost the Paraclete, be made in the name of the Holy Trinity. R̂. Amen.

Then he takes both vials of the said holy Oil and Chrism, and, pouring from both together in the form of a Cross, he says:

May this mixture of the Chrism of sanctification, and of the Oil of unction, and of the water of baptism, be made in the name of the Father, ✠ and of the Son, ✠ and of the Holy ✠ Ghost. R̂. Amen.

He then mixes the Oil with the water. If there are any to be baptized, he baptizes them in the usual way. (Blessing ends here when Baptistery is apart from the Church.)

After the blessing, the Baptismal Water is carried in Procession to the font in the following manner: the Thurifer leads, followed by the Subdeacon or Cleric with Cross, the Clergy, the Deacon carrying the Baptismal Water, and lastly the Celebrant. The Paschal Candle remains in its place; and meanwhile the following Canticle is sung.

(If there are no Deacon and Subdeacon, the Procession proceeds in the following manner: Thurifer, Cross-bearer and servers, then one of the servers carrying the Baptismal Water, and the Celebrant.)

Canticle. *Ps. 41, 2-4.* As the hart pants after the fountain of water, so my soul pants after Thee, O God. V̂. My soul has thirsted for the living

God: when shall I come and appear before the face of God. ℣. My tears have been my bread day and night, whilst it is said to me daily: Where is thy God?

After the blessed water is poured into the font, he says:

℣. The Lord be with you. ℟. And with thy spirit.

Let us pray. Almighty and everlasting God, look mercifully on the devotion of Thy people desiring a new birth, who, like the hart, seek after the fountain of Thy waters; and mercifully grant that the thirst of their faith may, by the Sacrament of Baptism, sanctify their souls and bodies. Through our Lord, etc. ℟. Amen.

He incenses the font. Then all return in silence to the sanctuary for the Renewal of Baptismal Promises.

Renewal of Baptismal Promises

The Celebrant, laying aside his purple vestments, puts-on white stole and cope; then, putting incense into the thurible, he incenses the Paschal Candle. Standing in front of the Paschal Candle in the middle of the sanctuary, or in the ambo or the pulpit, he begins as follows:

Dearly beloved brethren, on this most holy night, holy Mother the Church, calling to mind the death and burial of our Lord Jesus Christ, keeps a vigil for Him, returning love for love; she rejoices exceedingly, while celebrating His glorious Resurrection.

But since, as the Apostles teach, we have been buried with Christ by baptism unto death, we also must walk in the newness of life, just as Christ has arisen from the dead; knowing that the old man in us has been crucified along with Christ, so that we may no longer serve sin. Therefore, let us realize that we are dead to sin, but alive unto God, in Christ Jesus our Lord.

Wherefore, dearly beloved brethren, now that the Lenten exercises have been accomplished, let us renew the promises of holy Baptism, by which we formerly renounced Satan and his works, as well as the world, which is at enmity with God; and let us promise to serve God faithfully in the Holy Catholic Church. Therefore:

Priest: Do you renounce Satan?

People: We do renounce him.

Priest: And all his works?

People: We do renounce them.

Priest: And all his display?

People: We do renounce it.

Priest: Do you believe in God, the Father almighty, Creator of heaven and earth?

People: We do believe.

Priest: Do you believe in Jesus Christ, His only Son, our Lord, Who was born into this world and suffered for us?

People: We do believe.

Priest: And do you believe in the Holy Ghost, the Holy Catholic Church, the communion of Saints, the forgiveness of sins, the resurrection of the body, and life everlasting?

People: We do believe.

Priest: Now let us pray all together, as our Lord Jesus Christ taught us to pray.

People: Our Father, etc.

Priest: And may almighty God, the Father of our Lord Jesus Christ, Who has given us a new birth by means of water and the Holy Spirit, and forgiven all our sins, preserve us by His grace in the same Christ Jesus our Lord unto life everlasting.

People: Amen.

The Celebrant sprinkles the people with holy water taken from the container used in the blessing of Baptismal Water; or, if there has been no blessing of Baptismal Water, he uses "ordinary" holy water.

The above allocution and Renewal of Baptismal Promises may be spoken in the vernacular anywhere in the world, as long as the text is approved by the Ordinary.

The Second Part of the Litany of the Saints

After the Renewal of Baptismal Promises, the Cantors (or the Celebrant himself), sing the second part of the Litany, while all kneel and make the responses.

The Celebrant and Ministers go to the sacristy and put on white vestments for the celebration of Solemn Mass.

(When there are no Deacon and Subdeacon, the Celebrant and servers go to the sacristy where the Celebrant puts on white vestments and servers put on festal vestments for the celebration of Solemn Mass. But if there are no Cantors, the Celebrant himself sings the Litany, and at its conclusion goes to the sacristy with the servers to put on vestments for Solemn Mass, as described above.)

In the meantime, the Paschal Candle is fixed in its own candelabrum at the Gospel side, and the Altar is prepared for Solemn Mass, with lighted candles and flowers.

Propítius esto, *parce nobis, Dómine.*	Be merciful to us: *spare us, O Lord.*
Propítius esto, *exáudi nos, Dómine.*	Be merciful to us: *graciously hear us, O Lord.*
Ab omni malo,*	From all evil,*
Ab omni peccáto,	From all sin,
A morte perpétua,	From everlasting death,
Per mystérium sanctæ incarnatiónis tuæ,	Through the mystery of Thy holy incarnation,
Per advéntum tuum,	Through Thy coming,

Líbera nos, Dómine.

Deliver us, O Lord.

Per nativitátem tuam,* | Through Thy nativity,*

Per baptísmum, et sanctum jejúnium tuum, | Through Thy baptism and holy fasting,

Per crucem, et passiónem tuam, | Through Thy Cross and passion,

Per mortem, et sepultúram tuam, | Through Thy death and burial,

Per sanctam resurrectiónem tuam, | Through Thy holy resurrection,

Per admirábilem ascensiónem tuam, | Through Thy admirable ascension,

Per advéntum Spíritus Sancti Parácliti, | Through the coming of the Holy Spirit, the Comforter,

In die judícii, | In the day of judgment,

Peccatóres,** | We sinners,**

Ut nobis parcas, | That Thou spare us,

Ut Ecclésiam tuam sanctam régere, et conserváre dignéris, | That Thou vouchsafe to rule and preserve Thy holy Church,

Ut domnum apostólicum, et omnes ecclesiásticos órdines in sancta religióne conserváre dignéris, | That Thou vouchsafe to preserve Thy apostolic prelate, and all ecclesiastical orders in holy religion,

Ut inimícos sanctæ Ecclésiæ humiliáre dignéris, | That Thou vouchsafe to humble the enemies of Thy holy Church,

Ut régibus et princípibus christiánis pacem, et veram concórdiam donáre dignéris, | That Thou vouchsafe to grant peace and true concord to Christian kings and princes,

Ut nosmetípsos in tuo sancto servítio confortáre, et conserváre dignéris, | That Thou vouchsafe to confirm and preserve us in Thy holy service,

Ut ómnibus benefactóribus nostris sempitérna bona retríbuas, | That Thou render eternal good things to all our benefactors,

*Líbera nos, Dómine.
**Te rogámus, audi nos.

*Deliver us, O Lord.
**We beseech Thee, hear us.

Ut fructus terræ dare, et conserváre dignéris,*	That Thou vouchsafe to give and preserve the fruits of the earth,*
Ut ómnibus fidélibus defúnctis réquiem ætérnam donáre dignéris,	That Thou vouchsafe to give eternal rest to all the faithful departed,
Ut nos exaudíre dignéris,	That Thou vouchsafe graciously to hear us,
Agnus Dei, qui tollis peccáta mundi, *parce nobis, Dómine.*	Lamb of God, Who takest away the sins of the world, *spare us, O Lord.*
Agnus Dei, qui tollis peccáta mundi, *exáudi nos, Dómine.*	Lamb of God, Who takest away the sins of the world, *graciously hear us, O Lord.*
Agnus Dei, qui tollis peccáta mundi, *miserére nobis.*	Lamb of God, Who takest away the sins of the world, *have mercy on us.*
Christe, audi nos.	Christ, hear us.
Christe, exáudi nos.	Christ, graciously hear us.

Te rogámus, audi nos.	*We beseech Thee, hear us.*

EASTER VIGIL MIDNIGHT MASS

At the end of the Litany, the Cantors (or Choir) solemnly intone the "Kyrie eleison," as usual. Meanwhile the Celebrant, with his Ministers, in white vestments, comes to the foot of the Altar and makes the proper reverence, omitting the prayers at the foot of the Altar. Ascending, he kisses the Altar and incenses it in the usual way. When the Choir finishes the "Kyrie," the Celebrant solemnly intones the "Gloria," and the bells, which have remained silent, are now rung again, and the statues and sacred images are uncovered. Turning to the people, he says:

℣. The Lord be with you. ℞. And with thy spirit. ⌐

Prayer. O God, Who dost illumine this most holy night by the glory of the Lord's Resurrection, preserve in the new children of Thy family the spirit of adoption which Thou hast given; that, renewed in body and mind, they may render to

Thee a pure service. Through the same, etc. ℞. Amen. ⇒

Epistle. *Col. 3, 1-4*. Brethren: If you have risen with Christ, seek the things that are above, where Christ is seated at the right hand of God. Mind the things that are above, not the things that are on earth. For you have died and your life is hidden with Christ in God. When Christ, your life, shall appear, then you too will appear with Him in glory.

At the end of the Epistle, the Celebrant sings "Alleluia" three times, each time in a higher tone, and all present repeat after him in the same tone as the Celebrant. Then the Choir continues with the following:

℣. *Ps. 117, 1*. Give praise to the Lord, for He is good: for His mercy endures forever.

℣. *Ps. 116, 1-2*. O praise the Lord, all ye nations; and praise Him, all ye people. ℣. For His mercy is confirmed upon us: and the truth of the Lord remains forever.

At the Gospel, candles are not carried, but only incense.

● *Prayer: Cleanse My Heart, page 6.*

Gospel. *Matt. 28, 1-7*. Now late in the night of the Sabbath, as the first day of the week began to dawn, Mary Magdalene and the other Mary came to see the sepulchre. And behold, there was a great earthquake; for an angel of the Lord came down from heaven, and drawing near rolled back the stone, and sat upon it. His countenance was like lightning, and his raiment like snow. And for fear of him the guards were terrified, and became like dead men. But the angel spoke and said to the women, "Do not be afraid; for I know that you seek Jesus, Who was crucified. He is not here, for He has risen even as He said. Come, see the place where the Lord was laid. And go quickly, tell His disciples that He has risen, and behold, He goes before you into Galilee; there you shall see Him

Behold, I have foretold it to you." ℟. Praise be to Thee, O Christ.

Neither the Creed, nor the Offertory is said.

Secret. Accept, we beseech Thee, O Lord, the prayers of Thy people together with the sacrifice they offer, that what has been begun by the Easter mysteries, may by Thy working, profit us unto eternal healing. Through our Lord, etc. ⤸

Preface for Easter

℣. World without end. ℟. Amen. ℣. The Lord be with you. ℟. And with thy spirit. ℣. Lift up your hearts. ℟. We have lifted them up unto the Lord. ℣. Let us give thanks to the Lord, our God. ℟. It is fitting and just.

It is fitting indeed and just, right and helpful to salvation for us always to praise Thee, O Lord, but more gloriously on this night above others when Christ our Pasch was sacrificed. For He is the true Lamb Who has taken away the sins of the world: Who by dying has destroyed our death; and by rising again has restored us to life. And therefore with angels and archangels, with thrones and dominations, and with all the hosts of the heavenly army, we sing the hymn of Thy glory, evermore saying: Holy, Holy, Holy, etc., as on page 12.

After the distribution of Holy Communion, and the purification and ablution, Lauds is sung, as follows:

Ant. Alleluia, alleluia, alleluia.

Ps. 150. Praise the Lord in His sanctuary, praise Him in the firmament of His strength. Praise Him for His mighty deeds, praise Him for His sovereign majesty. Praise Him with the blast of the trumpet, praise Him with lyre and harp. Praise Him with timbrel and dance, praise Him with strings and pipe. Praise Him with sounding cymbals, praise Him with clanging cymbals. Let everything that has breath praise the Lord! Glory be to the Father, etc.

Ant. Alleluia, alleluia, alleluia.

Antiphon. And very early in the morning after the Sabbath, they came to the sepulcher at sunrise, alleluia. ➤

Benedictus. *Luke 1, 68-79.* Blessed be the Lord, the God of Israel, because He has visited and wrought redemption for His people, and has raised up a horn of salvation for us, in the house of David His servant, as He promised through the mouth of His holy ones, the prophets from of old; salvation from our enemies, and from the hand of all who hate us, to show mercy to our forefathers and to be mindful of His holy covenant, of the oath that He swore to Abraham our father, that He would grant us, that, delivered from the hand of our enemies, we should serve Him without fear, in holiness and justice before Him all our days. And thou, child, shalt be called the prophet of the Most High, for thou shalt go before the face of the Lord to prepare His ways, to give to His people knowledge of salvation through forgiveness of their sins, because of the loving-kindness of our God, wherewith the Orient from on high has visited us, to shine on those who sit in darkness and in the shadow of death, to guide our feet into the way of peace. Glory be, etc.

Antiphon. And very early in the morning, etc.

℣. The Lord be with you. ℟. And with thy spirit. ➤

Postcommunion. Pour forth upon us, O Lord, the Spirit of Thy love, that those whom Thou hast filled with the Easter sacraments may, by Thy goodness, be of one mind. Through our Lord in the unity of the same Holy Spirit, God.

℣. The Lord be with you. ℟. And with thy spirit.

The Deacon (or Celebrant) turns to the people and says:

℣. Go, you are dismissed. Alleluia, alleluia.

℟. Thanks be to God. Alleluia, alleluia.

The Blessing is given, the Gospel of St. John is omitted, and all return to the sacristy.

Made in the USA
Monee, IL
27 March 2024

55819889R00075